Disaster Survival!

James Evans Sr.

Disaster Survival!

What Do We Really Need To Survive!

Foreword

First this is not a book on poaching, or a wilderness survival book, it's not even a book about surviving a natural or unnatural disasters. However, it could be used for all of these conditions

I don't believe in pouching as a commercial enterprise or if you have enough money to feed your family, yes I have pouched from time to time but only when I couldn't afford to feed my family. That was went I lived in Pickle Lake, Northern Ontario.

So, now this is me trying to write down all the crap I know have seen, heard or have done in my life for my kids and grandkids!

For me the downside of writing this book is that it's all been written about before and there are tons of books out there right now to prove it! However, my kids are lazy and want it all in one place so here goes!

I was born in Sept. on the 9th day of 1953 in the city of London Ontario Canada. However, my story really doesn't start until Oct 16, 1962 just a little more than a month passed my 9th birthday. That was the year I learned that my government and any other government didn't care about people like you and I.

That was the year of the Cuban Missile Crisis 13 days of fear of the kind I have never experienced before or since!

The United States of America and the USSR were in a nuclear standoff over Cuba. Both counties had their fingers on the nuclear trigger with us average people caught in the middle.

TV with aircraft footage, radio, news paper reports and everyone else, all thinking the world was going to end in a nuclear fireball.

I wanted to live, I wanted my mom and dad, and my friends to live, but what can I do what could I do?

I made myself a promise that if I lived, I was never going to be caught again, unprepared never ever again! So with that promise to myself, my childhood was over I set out to try and be prepared to survive anything.

The change that came over me was to say the least, was dramatic. I stopped going to the movies with my friends I also stopped buying candy at the corner store.

Disaster Survival!

As a young boy I had problems reading, it turns out I was dyslexic. Okay, what is dyslexia? It's a general term for disorders that involves difficulty in learning to read or interpret words, letters, and other symbols, but that does not affect general intelligence.

I will never forget all the long hours that my mom and I spent helping me learn to read and understand what it was I was reading.

"Thank you mom for all your love, understanding and your attention as long as I live I will never forget you and all you have done for me!"

The proof is in the pudding they say and that proof came in my high school years when a teacher (Mr. Penny my science teacher in Stephenville Newfoundland) said to my mom "that my reading and word comprehension were at a 2nd year university level, and I could talk intelligently on any subject." However, I still can't spell worth a dam so how funny is that!

Mr. Penny was always giving us little trick questions to see if we could figure out the right answer. Here's the one that stands out the most for me. Let's see if you can figure it out!

Which is heavier a pound of lead or a pound of gold? Remember this is a trick question, but not the one you may think it is. The class and I had a lively debate all of them saying a pound is a pound except for me. I said that a pound of lead was heavier than a pound of gold.

As you can imagine the other students tried to point out to me just how wrong I was. After about 5 minutes without the class changing my mind Mr. Penny ended the debate by asking me why I thought that a pound of lead was heavier than a pound of gold.

Has anyone reading this, figured it out yet? Gold is measured in troy weigh with only 12 ounces to a pound not 16 ounces like lead that uses the standard 16 ounces to the pound.

Your mind is your best survival tool so use it wisely. Don't follow others blindly just because everyone else thinks their right.

So how does a 9 year old with dyslexia and problems learning to read and understanding what he is reading change so much?

Well, as I learned to read I started to understand that **"Everything man has done, everything he is doing now, and everything he will do in the future will be written down somewhere".** I knew this was how I was going to keep that promise to myself. **Knowledge is Power!**

So to everyone I say this, if you can learn only one thing in life, learn to read well and understand what it is you're reading. If you learn this simple lesson, you can teach yourself anything and everything that the world has to offer.

Remember I said I stopped going to the movies and buying candies so what did a 9 year old spend his weekly allowance on? Books, books and more books!

The first books I bought were books on guns, then books on hunting and trapping, also magazines like, Soldier Of Fortune, Popular Science, Popular Mechanics and the list grew from there.

I sent away to the ads in the back of those books (no internet back then) and magazines. I got military manuals on survival, cold weather survival, desert survival, jungle survival, how to survive at sea, nuclear survival, and navigation on land or sea.

I got military manuals on small unit tactics and training, on shooting, sniper manuals, military manuals on explosives and improvised explosives (how to make your own explosives in the field using what you have on hand), booby traps not to be confused with, today's IED's which are Improvised explosive devices. Booby traps are devices that wound without killing and without explosives. Some did kill.

The idea behind booby traps of old was that wounding was better than killing and it instills fear in your enemy. It will take one or two men out of action to help this one wounded man a dead soldier would be left behind for others to pick up at a later time and did not slow down the advance of the patrol. It also uses up more of your enemies' resources to care for him. In the long run you don't have to kill to win. (Vietnam War)

I was learning all this, years before any survival book ever hit the bestseller list with authors that I can't ever remember today. My kids have told me I was probably one of the first and youngest survivalist and I should write my own book. I'm 64 years young now and there's no way I'll ever get to write it all down.

So, let's get on with what I want to teach my kids and grandkids.

Chapter 1

Survival Books, Videos, and TV Shows

All books, Videos, and TV shows have their own idea of the best way to survive a worldwide disaster/pandemic or a local disaster and this book is no different from them. I would like to quote Clint Eastwood in the (Dirty Harry movie)"opinions are like assholes, everybody got one" so here is mine. (My opinion not my asshole LOL)

When it comes to survival books, videos, and TV shows there are five types, there are the ones with money (there are two subgroups here) concentrating on buying land that is off the grid or buying abandoned missile silos, or building bunkers. Stocking them with everything money can buy with the intentions of rebuilding after a worldwide disaster, maybe even set themselves up as the new leaders or they may just wait for a new or the old government to be reestablished.

The second type are (the bug out) ones, the ones that will grab their survival packsacks and head for the hill. They intend to come out of the hills when things have settled down and will form small bands of survivors. They also intend to live off the land for an extended period of time. Theses, people will be mostly families and close friends.

The third type are (the bug in) ones, Just like the bug out type the only difference here is that they intend to stay put in the city or the town that they are living in.

The fourth type is the totally unprepared and here there are two subgroups as well. The honest people and the criminal element that didn't see it coming until it was too late.

The fifth type will be what's left of the military and the police forces.

All these groups will have lots in common. In general, they will all have leaders and followers, honest and dishonest people, religious and non-religious people. People with special skills like doctors, lawyers, construction works and so on.

Disaster Survival!

So which of the five groups have the best chance for survival and which has the least chance?

Personally, I think if you can stick your head up out of the rubble and say what the hell just happened you now have a 50% chance at survival your chances go up or down now depending on what you do next!

Homesteading VS Silos/Bunkers

So let's have a closer look at the rich or semi rich the group that bought the land to bug out too, or just live on, it before the worldwide disaster. Don't confuse these people, with the backpack bug out group they are not the same and I'll get to that later.

If you have been reading carefully, you should have seen that there are two subgroups here. However, both will start out the same.

They will both have the central group of family and friends that start out together, to do the planning and pick the land. They may have the necessary funds to buy the land, outright or they may need to recruit others of like minded people to help buy the land.

One group will live on the land on weekends bringing in supplies and building up their new homestead. The other group will have the money or the means to live on the land right away and will go to the nearest town to bring in more supplies as needed.

That will be the only difference between the two groups. Both groups would build the buildings they needed. Clear the ground for planting crops and pastureland for any livestock they would need. The livestock would be horses, cows, sheep, pigs, chickens and the like with more building to house and care for them. Hunting, fishing and trapping would help supplement their food stores.

For electrical power a combination of gas/diesel powered generators with wind/solar and water power systems.

For the defense of the homestead fences, lookout towers, and weapons would round this out to being a nice place to live and survive.

The only real problems would be in the leadership and how well the followers would/could work together. Most followers would have their own pet projects and may not want to delay them just to help work on someone else's

God help them all if they elect a dictatorship style leader like Jim Jones or David Koresh, this would also be problematic for any survival group. If you don't know who these two men are then do a Google search and find out!

Silos/Bunkers

Now the Missile silo/bunker group with their harden sites and all their resources set to last for anywhere from six months to six years would stay safe. Well, you may think so, but bad leadership could doom them. Also, many people living in a confined space you have the added problem of claustrophobia or just getting on each other's nerves. If they picked people unknown to them you will have personality problems that could/would end in violence.

This is why NASA and other groups have very strict screening procedures for people that will spend a long time on space flights, such as on the international space station or living on the moon or mars.

Let's say that everything worked out for them and they survive to re-enter a world that has been devastated by a worldwide disaster. With their resources gone or almost gone, they will have to scavenge, just like the rest of humanity that had survived on the outside.

If they spent the time in confinement to study fishing, hunting, trapping and farming then their chances are good that that some or all may survive. However, if they did the normal things, like eating, sleeping, and raising their families, they're going to have major problems on the outside especially if the government didn't get reestablished yet.

Disaster Survival!

Even if they had lots of guns and ammo they will be like babies in the woods. They will need help from good people or bad to survive without it they will fall prey to other criminal elements still roaming around.

This to me looks like a classic example of resources being the enemy of creative thinking.

Your mind is your best survival tool so use it. To me this is just the opposite of thinking head, where people think that resources alone will save the day.

If I had a choice, I think I would pick the homesteaders if I had the money.

Bugging Out VS Bugging In

Bugging out can take many forms, but they all have the same theme get out of the city/town and head for the hills. Well, not just the hills they will have a predetermined area to go to like a lake, a cabin or a small farm somewhere they think is secluded and safe.

In a lot of respects this looks like an average man's idea of a temporary homestead used for emergencies only. They may also be used from time to time as a holiday getaway. Like a week at the cottage they would not have livestock or farmland, but would have some food, water and other supplies.

There will be some people that will go it alone just grabbing their survival bug out bag and their favorite survival book and go. This is an extreme example, but they do have a chance just look at history.
There have been recent examples of a kid in a downed plane surviving in the wilderness until he was rescued. Small children lost for days or weeks, others at sea and they survived so it's not impossible just dammed hard and you need a lot of luck.

Sometimes it's better to be lucky than good just keeping using your head when all else seems lost!

Bugging In

Bugging in is the idea of hiding in plain sight with two weeks or more of food and water. This can be accomplished by making your home look like its deserted and already been looted. It can also be accomplished by making your house look like it's a contaminated area with some kind of Biohazard or by using both methods.

You will need to plan ahead and get some Biohazard signs saying, contaminated area do not enter, tape saying to not cross contaminated area and the like, from a joke shop or make your own. The best way to find signs of this nature is at Halloween.

If you can't find any get a can of red spray paint. Spray the front and back of your house with a skull and crossbones and write contaminated area do not enter under it.

Throw out some trash, maybe a chair, a lamp, an old mattress; things that will look like the CDC (Center for Disease Control) may have thrown out.

Board up the windows on the ground floor from the outside and loosely board up the front and back doors with two planks of wood in an x shape. This is so, if you need to go out you still can.

Cover the inside of the windows with heavy blankets so when you use a candle or turn on a flashlight, it won't be seen from outside. Now you hide and hope that the rioters and looters can read and are too afraid to look inside.

Totally Unprepared

Most people will fall into this category and most will not survive but some will. Why will most die in a worldwide disaster? They will die in riots over food and water and shot by the police and military as looters. Some will die at the hands of criminals or other desperate people for what little food or water or anything else of value they may have.

Not all of these people will be criminals just people caught in a bad situation with no way out. The lucky ones who keep their heads will find ways of hiding and avoiding the chaos.

Disaster Survival!

It's my guess that after the about two or three weeks of rioting, looting, murdering, gang wars, rape and fires the military and police will have most, but not all under some kind of shaky control.

The Military and the Police

As the things start to go bad the police will be on the front lines. They will be overwhelmed by the magnitude of the job. The military will be called in to take over the job with the police in a support role.

The police and the military will start to take heavy losses as the rioters get more organized and fight back this will be mostly from the criminal gangs.

There will be some military and police that will leave their units to go and be with their families, others that will just go rouge for whatever reason.

Eventually the cities will start to settle down with different factions holding on to the areas they have. These areas will be held by warlords, some will be good others not so good.

This may be hard to understand until you look at the Middle East and Africa, and how the warlords there have divided up the cities in the past civil wars.

What about the government? Did you think I forgot about them? Well, the government will be hiding in their bunkers just like the group of silo people.

The difference here is they will still be trying to tell us how to fix the mess the world is in. Their first orders will be to call for martial law and curfews and set up refugee camps and compounds.

Again, I draw your attention to the Middle East and Africa and the refugee camps and compounds there. Are these people safe and do they have lots of food and water?

Not even close and that's with millions of tons of supplies, being sent to them year after year from the rest of the world. Supplies like, food, water, clothes, and blanket ECT.

In a worldwide disaster, they will not be supplied by, other friendly countries.

I would sooner have the illusion of freedom and take my chances on my own. I believe it would be better than fighting for the scraps that find there, way into those refugee camps and compounds.

One last thing I should say is that the city will have dead bodies, most likely lots of them. The dead are still a real threat to the living; you will need to burn or dig big holes for mass graves to prevent disease.

I hope you didn't think I was talking about them becoming zombies/walkers. Some days it's better not to have my kids reading over my shoulder, they come up this the craziest ideas from watching too much TV.

However, if the dead, do come back to life the standard practice here is to shoot them in the head, this will also stop the living, really!

Chapter 2

The Three Rules of Survival

The first thing you should know is the rule of three, Three minutes without air, three days without water and three weeks without food will usually end with your death. I say usually because there are always exceptions to the rules. For instance, some people can hold their breath for a hell of a lot longer than 3 minutes! So the rule of three is just a basic guideline to remember.

Just recently I have been seeing internet survivalist saying food is not that essential as you can last weeks without food. Not only is this wrong its dangers thinking after a week with little or no food your body will start to break down body fat, muscles, and other internal organs to sustain itself. You will become weaker, disoriented, and depressed less able to move around looking for water and food. Try to eat at least one meal every day or two so you can keep your strength up and be thinking clearly. **Food is essential if you become too weak and disoriented from hunger, to find water, you will die of thirst before you die of hunger!**

Never *Ever!* Waste Any Natural Resource! If you kill it, eat it!

Check your local laws before you try anything written here! Don't break the law! If you do, don't get caught! If you get caught don't call me! I've warned you!

Survival is a mindset you can have all the survival gear you want, but if you don't have the will to survive it won't do you any good! You should also know how to use your gear, fix it, find replacement parts, or how to improvise parts or stuff you don't have!

I heard someone on television say once that, three hours without shelter would lead to your death as part of the rule of three maybe he was adding to the list I don't know?

Yes, shelter is important, but except for very extreme conditions would it ever kill you in three hours if you don't have any.

I've no idea about what the guy had in mind when he said that three hours without shelter would kill Maybe he was thinking about, say, radioactive fallout, breathing in volcanic ash, or maybe being buck naked in a blizzard who knows? I do know one thing, being buck naked in a blizzard; miles from any shelter will definitely kill you in less than three hours, go figure?

There is another group of three that all animals need, it's a triangle of life kind of thing and they all need it including us. All animals need water, food, and a safe place to sleep.

Deer and Moose will leave tracks in the woods that can be followed, but be aware so do trains and you could follow train tracks all day and not find a train! You would be better off to get a good map and find out where the lakes, ponds and rivers are. That's where you will find the game.

If you're hungry, lakes and rivers are the best places to find food and the easiest food to get are the fish. In North America all freshwater fish are eatable, but you have to be careful about polluted water. So before I get into fishing I'd like to talk a little about disasters and survival

What Do We Really Need To Survive!

You need water, food, and shelter! Your most precious survival tool is your mind, so don't lose it!

So what else will we need? Let's have a reality check, how many of us do you think will ever be caught buck naked in blizzard miles away from shelter? If any of you said any number other than zero, all I can say is what kind of lifestyle are you living? Really, even the most diehard nudist puts on clothes when it gets cold outside!

Disaster Survival!

With that in mind do we really need to learn how to flint nape stone tools and weapons learn how to tan animal hides for clothes or start a fire by rubbing two sticks together?

Just so you know I tried to use a hand fire drill and I blistered my hands and it felt like they were going to catch fire instead of the wood.

The wood well, I did make a small amount of smoke! Yes, I've even tried the fire bow using one of my shoelaces. After spending most of the day I did start a fire!! YAY FOR ME! If I were really in a survival situation, I would have eaten my catch raw way before I started that fire!

Do yourself a favor and go to your nearest hunting store; they all carry flint striker type fire starters! Most are small and cost less the $20 dollars. By small I mean you can put them on your keychain or on a belt loop of your pants. Some even have a magnesium block with a flint striker built into it.

With that one you can make a hot fire fast, even with damp wood and tinder! Even the biggest of them will fit into your pocket or purse. So get three or four and put them in your pocket, on your keychain, in your fanny pack, and your packsack!

As for tools and clothes, hell you will be able to find them all over the place. Really, just look at any hardware store or a shopping mall and think how many people one of these could supply?

Okay, I'm not talking about looting the stores! Looting to me is taking things like radios, TVs, laptops, and cell phones things you don't need to survive. Scavenging to me is about getting the things that will keep you alive a little longer like water, food, some tools, maps, clothes and a first aid kit. The truth is, it's all stealing, no matter how you look at it. If I had to go to court after a disaster for stealing, then I would rather it be for stealing food and water and not for a T.V. and a stereo. I really hope you can see the differences between the two!

So what do we really need to learn? You need to learn how to find and catch fish and animals by fishing, hunting and trapping. We need to learn to find shelter or make some. You will also need to learn how to get out of a city by the fastest and safest

route possible. You need to look at everyday things in a new light, Can I eat it, or can I use it in some way to catch food or carry water and other supplies.

Take this information use it as a starting point. Nothing here is written in stone take it apart rearrange it, add to it. Life and survival is one big puzzle some pieces will fit in many different places to make something new. Never stop thinking, never stop improvising, and never stop trying to create something new out of what you have on hand!

Chapter 3

Cities: Staying VS: Leaving?

Here we have a multitude of problems and everyone will need to evaluate them for themselves! No, I'm not going to leave you hanging; I'll go over some of your options.

If you get a severe weather warning that's saying you should evacuate and have a vehicle, then go, get out of the area and don't be the last one to leave! No vehicle? Be the first in line for any civil evacuation to the nearest safe zone! The best way to survive a disaster any disaster is not to be there when it happens!

Okay for some reason known only to you, you're one of the last to leave. Yes, it happens all the time as everyone can't be first and I understand this! So here you are last or next to last and the exit roads from the city have all been turned into one long parking lot.

I see this on the news after every major disaster like Katrina with helicopter news footage. The helicopter news reports also show all the inbound lanes to the city are totally empty? Well, maybe with only one or two vehicles going into the city.

I have to shake my head and wonder why this is happening. Sure, they are needed for disaster relief efforts, but all the inbound lanes? This is just poor civil evacuation planning, you only need one inbound lane for relief efforts as lots of it will be done by airlifting helicopters, and if the airports are still working then by military transport planes as well.

In most of the cases I've seen the inbound and outbound lanes are separated by a grassy strip of land. You do know that they are smooth enough to drive on, right?

They are used for traffic accidents it gives rescue trucks and the police a way to get past any traffic jams so they can get in and do their jobs.

Oh my god, I can hear all the law abiding citizens screaming at me, it's against the law to drive on them you fool! Well, go ahead and scream because driving on the wrong side of the road is against the law as well. However, if it saves my life and the lives of my family, I will gladly pay the fine and thank the judge as I pay for the ticket!

Something else you may not know, most countries, have a loophole in their laws and it goes like this.

In a life threatening situation and with justifiable reason people can break the law to save their life and the lives of others! I'm not saying you should go around breaking the law for fun or trying to exploit this loophole in the law!

Just look at some of the mass murder shooting sprees we have all seen on the news. If one of the soon to be a victim had managed to kill the crazed gunman. Do you think that person would be arrested for murder?

That's an extreme example of, **in a life threatening situation and with justifiable reason** to break the law. Not all situations will be that easy to justify so use your head and think! Always remember, your mind is your best survival tool so used it!

So now go get your maps and have a good look at them. Do you see the big high power electrical lines that come into the city to supply power to those big relay stations? You can use them to drive out of the city just don't run into them or damage them in any way. Take it slow going over the street curbs so you don't blow a tire or damage the underside of your vehicle.

You can also use the train tracks to get out of the city, again just go slow and stay out of the way of all trains! In most disasters the inbound trains will be order to stop. Also does you city have a river? Using a boat you could get out that way too.

What about commandeering a vehicle from the nearest used or new car lot? Wow, maybe in the case of a nuclear attack, an exploding volcano, an all-out nuclear meltdown of a Power station (the China syndrome), or an alien invasion.

Disaster Survival!

I think the answer here would be a definite yes! Maybe and maybe not for other types of disasters again, your mind is the best survival tool you have so used it!

Another problem is time and the number of people to evacuate. Most, if not all big cities have too many people to evacuate and never enough time to do it in. There are always those who will for one reason or another will be left behind.

Left Behind Now What?

We can't pick and chooses what disasters we want to come our way. Also, trying to prepare for every kind of disaster is almost impossible on a small budget or no budget at all.

Most natural disasters come with lots of shaking, high winds, and maybe high water and so on.

So where do you go to find shelter or do you stay in your apartment or home? I rent an older one story house made of wood that would never stand up in a hurricane or most other disasters. Also like most I don't have a vehicle to drive to safety so what should I do if I get left behind?

Well statistics show that reinforced steel and concrete buildings stand the best chance of not being destroyed in most natural disasters. Yes, great I hear you say, but which one do I choose?

If you're in a coastal city and a hurricane/typhoon is on the way head into the center of the city. Pick a tall reinforced steel and concrete building and hide in upper floors. If it's a nuclear attack, then head for the city's perimeter pick a two or three story reinforced steel and concrete building there.

Why? Well, in a hurricane/typhoon you want to be away from the coast and the tidal surge and the rest of the city will help slow and redirect the water down the side streets. This also may help lower the water level in your area and also help protect the building you're in.

With a nuclear attack the opposite is true get away from the city center and the airports get to the outskirts of the city and find a reinforced steel and concrete building there.

Why? Well the guys planning where the nuclear bombs will hit target those areas. Airports because they want to disrupt the air force and air traffic in the area and possibly destroy fighter jets and bombers on the ground. The city centers are targets because this will disrupt ground traffic, making it harder to move

around the country, helping the survivors and also moving supplies and troops to the needed areas.

Well, that's all nice and easy to understand I hear you say so how can I tell which buildings are concrete buildings and which are reinforced steel and concrete buildings? I'm not superman and don't have x-ray eyes, fool!

Well, I was getting to that so hang on and I'll tell you how you pushy little devils! LOL my kids are always looking over my shoulder to see what I am writing and asking questions!

A high rise and/or skyscraper have a steel inner core around the elevators and the outside walls are concrete with some steel supports that make them strong and light. Concrete and steel buildings are made with re-bar steel cages with the concrete poured into and around the cage. This kind of building has thick, heavy walls. Look at a five story standalone car parking structure or some big library builds even some government builds. Both car parking structures and big library buildings have to carry lots of weight (cars and books are heavy) and have to be extra strong, some of the government builds were made extra strong to be used as a bomb shelter.

Also for a nuclear attack the library basement is a very good place to hide as the book lined walls will help stop radiation from the blast from getting into the building (not as good as lead). If you're not killed by the blast, shock wave, or the heat wave, make your getaway by folding up your shirt and use that to breathe through like a face mask. This will catch a lot of radioactive dust that would otherwise get into your lungs. Oh, and it would also work for volcanic dust as well, it's not pretty, but it may help save your life. Now that I'm thinking about it you can use foam pillows and the like if you're at home or out and about.

Sudden Disasters

Sudden disasters are the ones that give you little or no warning at all, all you can do is hang on, say oh my god what's going on and we are all going to die! You get to scream and pray, and if you survive, it's just by plain dumb luck.

Some of these terrors that strike without warning are earthquakes, dams breaking, exploding volcanoes, Mud/land/snow slides/avalanches or a nuclear attack. If you're one of the lucky ones and can dig your way out you have a 50% chance at survival. The first thing is you may be in shock. You need to worry about yourself first and then others.

Give yourself the once over, do you have all your fingers and toes. Do you have any broken bones, cuts or burns take care of those things first! Your most precious survival tool is your mind, so don't lose it now!

There is no way to know how soon help will come maybe in minutes, hours or days or maybe not at all. You and any other survivors will have to work together so look around organizing and help each other! If your mind is your best survival tool, remember that two or more people working together will have a much better chance at survival.

The sad truth is there will be dead and those you can't help that will soon die without a doctor or a working hospital nearby. There is no way the average person will be prepared or can prepare for this. Just do what you can give them first aid and try to make them as comfortable as possible. Help may come, and you never know when, so it could save a life.

You need a to do list so first take care of yourself, then others, organize rescue teams and then a team to find water. I remember ether reading or hearing someone saying that water is the universal solvent. In a disaster, it should be right at the top of your list. Water to drink, water to clean cuts, water to clean bandages and the list goes on always be on the lookout for water! Be very careful if you light a fire to boil water or for heat there could be broken gas lines that could explode and create even more problems for you.

WATER, you may be able to scavenge water from nearby houses, apartments, or stores. Don't overlook any source of water. Believe it or not you can almost always find water in the bathrooms in any home or apartment. The tank on the back of toilets will have clean water in them that is used to flush the toilet bowl.

First, make sure that it doesn't have any cleaning agent in it. I'm talking about the urinal cakes and the blue stuff that disinfects and helps keep the toilet bowl clean! If it doesn't have anything like that than its good clean drinking water and you can use it. The same rules apply to the toilet bowl also be sure the water in the bowl is not yellow/brown or has any little logs floating it. If it's crystal clear water without a cleaning agent then it's also useable. Also the water pipes, hot water tanks, even the garden hose may have water still left in it.

The next thing you need to organize is teams to find food and shelter but in what order? That is going to depend on the situation you're in as to which is the most important were you in a blizzard, or is it a hurricane when the disaster happened. If yes, then shelter first if no then both are equally important after you have water, do both at the same time.

FOOD, finding food, you may be able to scavenge food from nearby houses, apartments, or stores.

I remember being at my grandparents' house in St. Johns Newfoundland when I was a very young boy. There was something I had never eaten before on my plate. I remember what it was now but didn't know back then, and I'll never forget what my grandmother said to me.

Her exact words were "boy, what doesn't kill will fatten" I had no idea then that she was talking about but I know now! I also remember asking her what this stuff was.

Disaster Survival!

Again, her reply was cryptic "boy, what the eyes don't see, the heart doesn't feel, just give it a taste you may like it, but you'll never know till you try it."

Well, I did try it and I did like it and after the meal was over she smiled and told me it was Seal meat. I've never been shy about tasting new foods after that.

My lesson is now yours to learn, there will be lots of new things for you to try to eat and you may not want to try them. Just remember my grandmother's words "what doesn't kill will fatten!"

It will also help when giving a person a new food item to eat and they ask what, is this you can tell them. What the eyes don't see, the heart doesn't feel just give it a taste you may like it, but you'll never know till you try it and you can tell them later what it was.

So what kinds of food will be available after the store bought food is eaten? Well, anything with feathers, fur, or scales to start with is eatable, some are tastier than others, but all will keep you alive.

This is just a short list of animals you may need to kill and eat and goes like this. Cats, dogs, birds, and rats all live in the city and there are lots of them.

If and when you get out of the city, food can be harder to find but may include deer, rabbit, bears, Moose and other big and small animals. If the city you're in has a river you could start fishing there first.

Chapter 4

Finding Fish without a Fish Finder

If you know that to look for, you can read a lake or river just like reading this book!

Okay, you're standing on the lake shore so what do you see? The people I've asked say things like, I can see the lake, waves on the water things of that nature. I see signs that say probable no fish here, maybe some fish here and others that say the fish are right here! Hey, stop laughing, there's no booze in my thermos and my cigarettes are just ordinary cigarettes!

I don't know the exact percentage, but if I have to make a guess I'd say about 75 to 80 percent of water in any given body of water (lake, river or ocean) won't attract and hold fish.

Have a look at a map of your country and look at there the cities are and how much land that has no town or city and you will see what I'm talking about. Why did people build cities and towns where they did? It was because of water, food, farm land or minerals in the ground!

Now, have you ever wondered why a prairie lake is so shallow when compared to a mountain lake? It's the terrain around the lake! The terrain doesn't stop at the water's edge it keeps on going down at the same slope rate, right to the bottom of the lake. So a gentle sloping land around a prairie lake just keeps going at the same rate. That's why you can walk out a hundred feet or so in a prairie lake and the water is still only waist deep.

A mountain lake has steep sloping sides of the mountains that make for deep cold lakes.

Prairie Lake

Okay, sure, you say, but where are the fish and don't tell me they're in the water!

Hold on finding fish is like opening a restaurant! It's all about location, location, location and we haven't looked at all the terrain in and around a lake yet!

Things like a finger of land sticking out into the lake or an island in the lake, a river entering the lake or one running out of the lake. Even bays, submerged sand bars, or large boulders. Everything plays a role in there the fish will be.

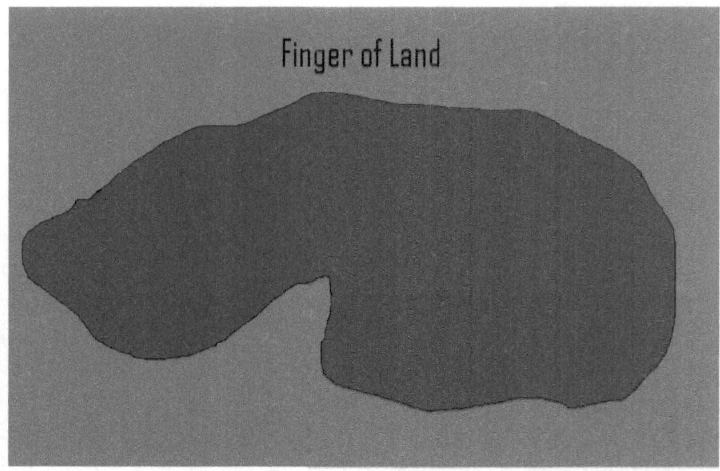

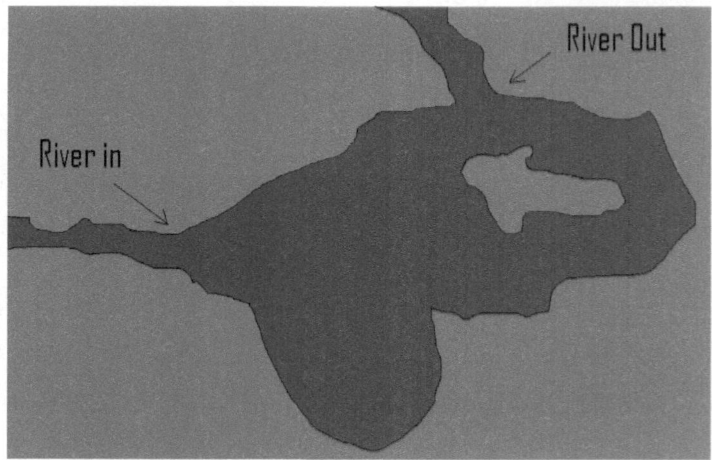

Alright, we've located lakes and we've located different structures in and around the lakes now it's time to find the fish. To understand where the fish will be we first have to understand the fish.

So what does a fish want? So do you remember the triangle of life water, food and shelter? Yep, that's what a fish wants! Waters not a problem the fish live in it and water in general is not going to help us find fish.

Disaster Survival!

Food and shelter are the things that will help us find the fish. To understand the behavior of fish we have to look at the lake/river as if it were in a house.

If we were in a house and there was a tornado heading for it what do people do? They run to the nearest window, maybe in the living room, the kitchen, the front or back door. Why, because it's natural to want to see the danger coming. Is the danger coming my way or not, if it's coming for them, they run for the basement to hide and to be safer!

Like all living things fish want to see the danger and evaluate it, is it a bear, human or something else. Is it coming my way, am I in danger? If the fish thinks it's in danger it makes a run for deeper water to be safer.

Okay, I don't think a fish can tell a human from a bear! It doesn't have to; it knows instinctively if it's in danger and will head for deeper water!

Deep water usually stays at a constant temperature and is not affected by air temperature. If the shallow water gets to hot or cold for the fish they will head for deeper water. Twice a year, once in the early summer and then in the fall every lake has a turnover. What this means is that all the water in the lake is at the same temperature. It's like stirring a pot of water and it's a good thing too! This turn over lets oxygen rich warm water and the cold oxygen depleted deep water mix. It also lets the fish go anywhere they like and it makes for a harder time finding them!

If you ever used a fish finder you may have seen fish hanging around the middle of the lake and way above the lake bottom. Well, now you know why.

Okay, let's see if we can find the fish now!

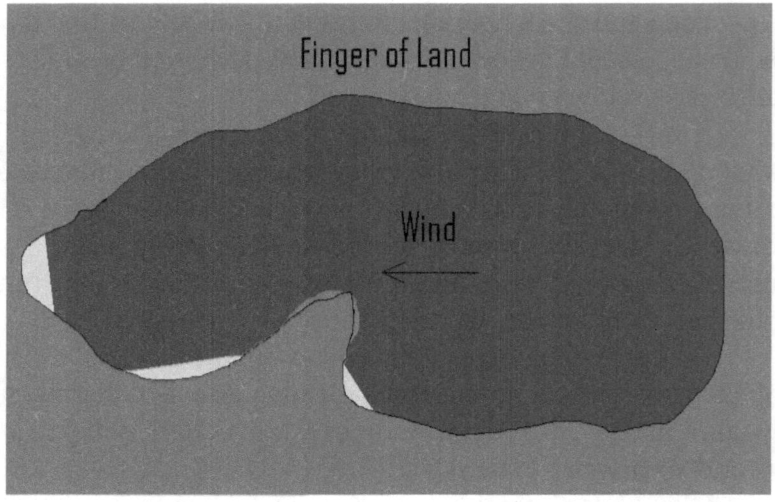

In the above picture we see a finger or point of land sticking out into the lake and an arrow indicating wind direction. Wind blowing across a body of water will create a wind induced current near the top of the lake. Fish like the walleye would take advantage of the land to stay out of the current. If any small bait fish like minnows got caught in the current it would pass by the point of land and the waiting walleye would slip out into the current for an easy meal. Depending on the wind direction the red zones show where the fish might be hiding.
Yes, I know the red zone is touching the green zone, but do you know why? The green is shallow water with weeds like cattails and things. The green zone is also a place where minnows and other small fish like to live. Big fish like to eat little fish. Large fish like the northern pike and others use the red zone as a safe highway from the deep water to the shallows and back again.

It's kind of like us going from the living room to the kitchen for a meal. So the green and red zones are the best places to find fish! Well, what about the green zone on the left side of the lake?

You can see the shoreline makes a large bay. If you follow the shoreline you can see other small bays I could have colored green as well.

Remember I said I see signs that say probable no fish here, maybe some fish here and others that say the fish are right here. To me that area says maybe some fish here.

What I can't see is a safe fish route to that bay from the deeper water. There may be an underwater structure that I can't see that the fish are using. The fish may have gotten there when the lake had a spring or fall turnover. I'm not saying there are no fish here.

To me, it's a maybe. If there are fish here, it's most likely their panfish, like sunfish and crappie, or bass, and northern pike.

If however you're looking for walleye or sauger then the place to be is the red and green structure combination.

Right, so how does a river flowing into or out of a lake affect the fish?

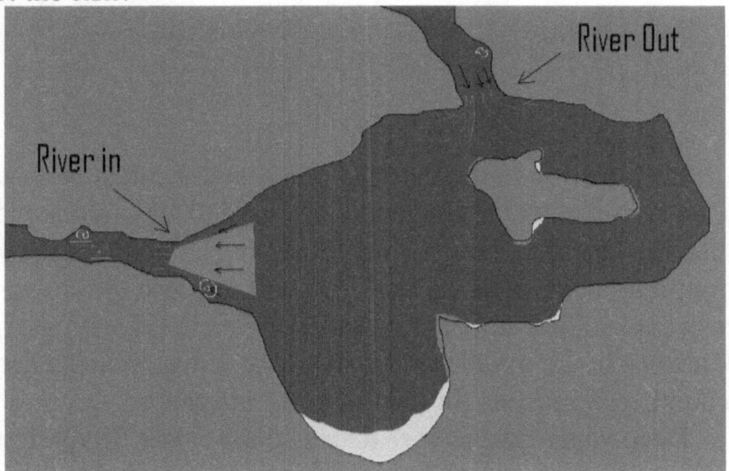

The red arrows indicate water direction. The white circles are back eddies and small whirlpools. The light brown is sediment from the river entering the lake. The black arrows indicate the direction the fish are facing and where you might find them. Fish always face into the current.

Just like the fish in the lake, river fish need some kind of structure to hide in, behind or beside to shelter them from the force of the river.

I like to fish where the river leaves the lake so I'm going to start there.

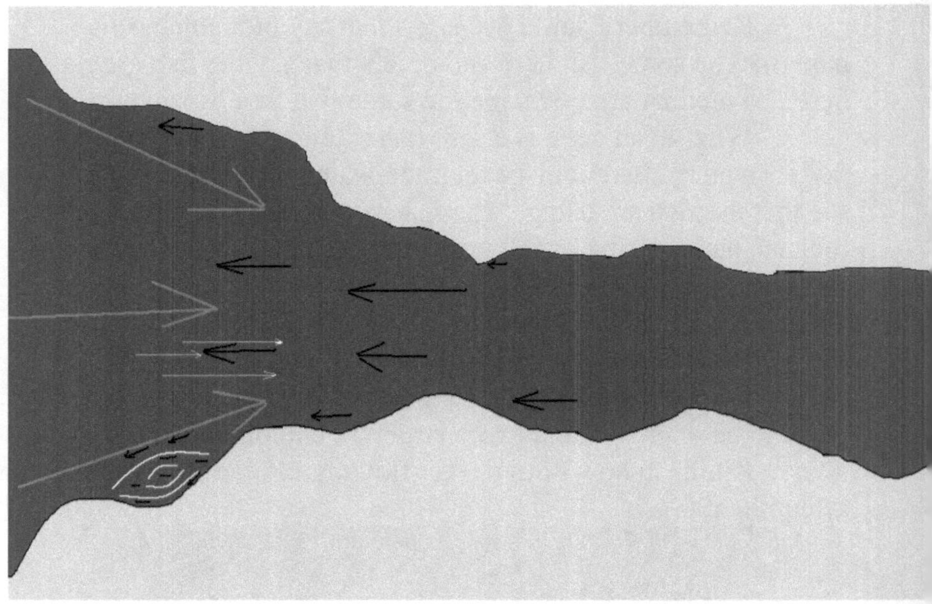

Let's start with the fact that fish like to be in slow water. Why, because, they don't have to work hard to stay in one place. Just like the lake fish, river fish will use fingers of shoreline what stick out into the river as shelter. Fish will also use the slower water in back eddies next to fast water for shelter. Okay, we have black arrows in the middle of the river that's that about? There are a number of reasons for the fish to be out there.

Deep water runs slower than shallow water. If you look at a river, sometimes you can see the lines were fast shallow water meets slow deep water. To the fish this dividing line is just like any other structure. The dividing line may look like, a line of foam on the water. The fish will swim in the slow water and dart out into the faster water for a meal as it passes them.

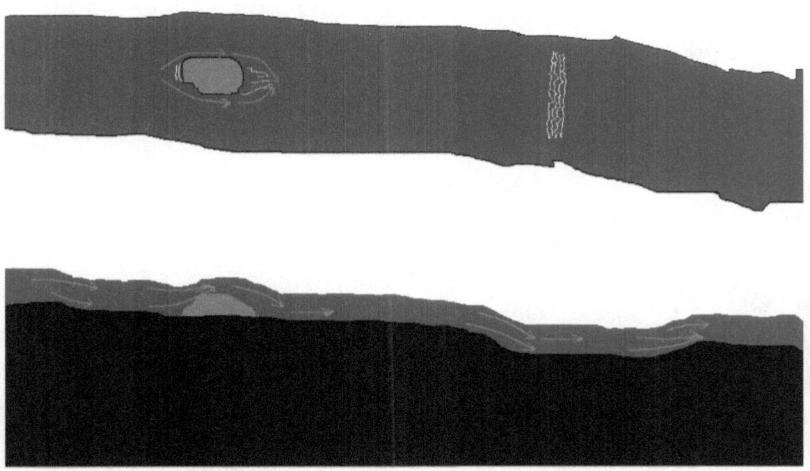

The top of the water that we see can tell us a lot about the bottom of the river. Underwater structure close to the surface causes the water to go up and over it and shows as rapids or a bulge. Water that looks smooth on the surface indicates a smooth bottom or maybe deep water if it's moving slow.

Fish, like rocks to hide behind, but they also can find slower water in front of and beside the rocks. It's not only rocks, sand bars, islands, bridge pilings old trees that have fallen into the river. Anything that can slow the water down and has been there for a while has a good chance of holding fish. Unfortunately, we have no way of seeing a hole in the river bottom. If there are potholes on the river bottom the fish will hide in them to get out of the main river current and could be anywhere in the river (a fish finder will show where they are.)

Think of a cold winter's day the wind is blowing hard and you're waiting for the bus. To get out of the wind you hide behind a telephone pole, mailbox anything to get out of the wind. When the bus does come you jump on and off you go to work or where ever.

For, the fish these slow water zones next to fast water is like you, sitting in a restaurant protected from the wind. The waiters/river carries the food passed you and all you/fish have to do is reach out and take what you want.

Think about it, if all you had to do in life was to sit around and have everything brought to you on a silver platter would you go somewhere else?

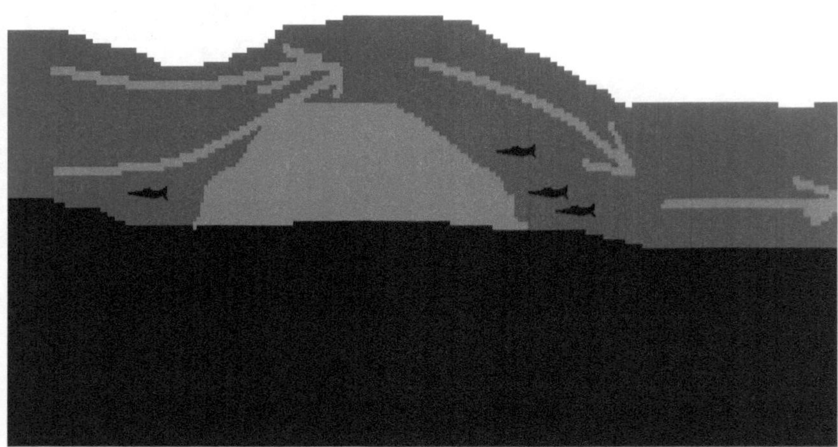

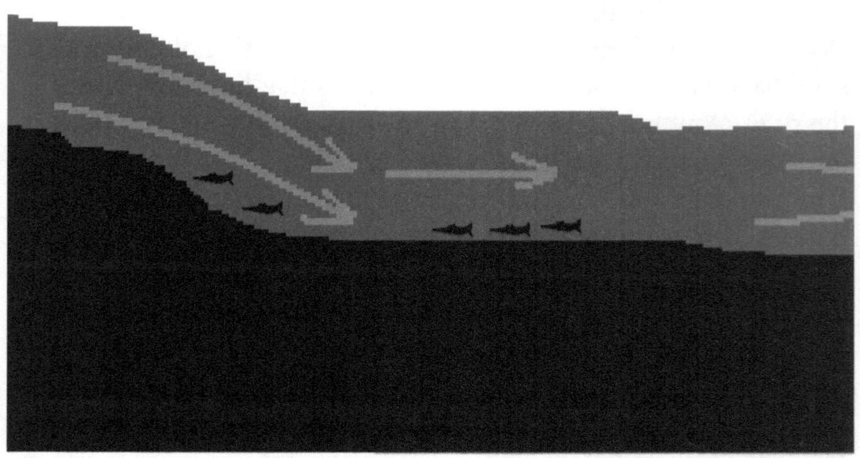

In the last three pictures you can see how the water contours the river bottom. A bend in a river can be a place to look for fish also.

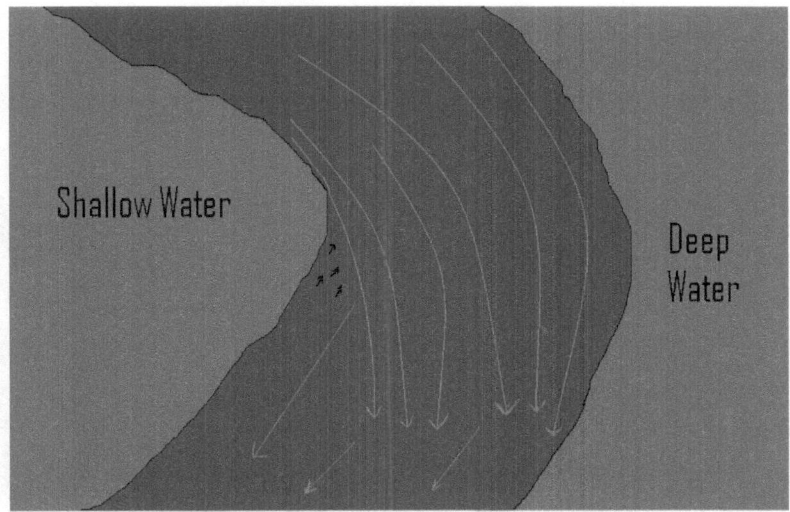

Water that is flowing doesn't want to turn it wants to continue in a straight line. An object in motion remains in motion unless acted upon by an outside force. (Do you remember that from high school science?) Water will always take the easiest route to lower ground. When a river is forced to make a bend the fast water on the outside bend digs, the riverbed, deeper. The water on the inside bend is forced to slow down for the curve and can't dig out the riverbed, so the water is shallower. Again fish will use the slow shallow water as a place to wait for food to be washed by them in the faster water.

Around and around the river flows and back to the lake the river must go! Well, unless it happens to empty into the ocean!

Rivers entering into a lake, creates a delta, the delta is made up of river sediment dropping out of the river when the river slows down. Like any structure fish will use it to their advantage looking for places to ambush the smaller fish.

Sometimes the river creates a mud line as well. A muddy river entering a clear lake will create a mud line, but sometimes a clear river in the spring flood or after a heavy rain can make them too. Lakes with wind driven waves hitting the lake shore can create them as well.

Larger fish will patrol this mud line looking for smaller fish to dart out of the mud line to feed on. To the larger fish this mud line is no different than a weed line separating weeds from open water.

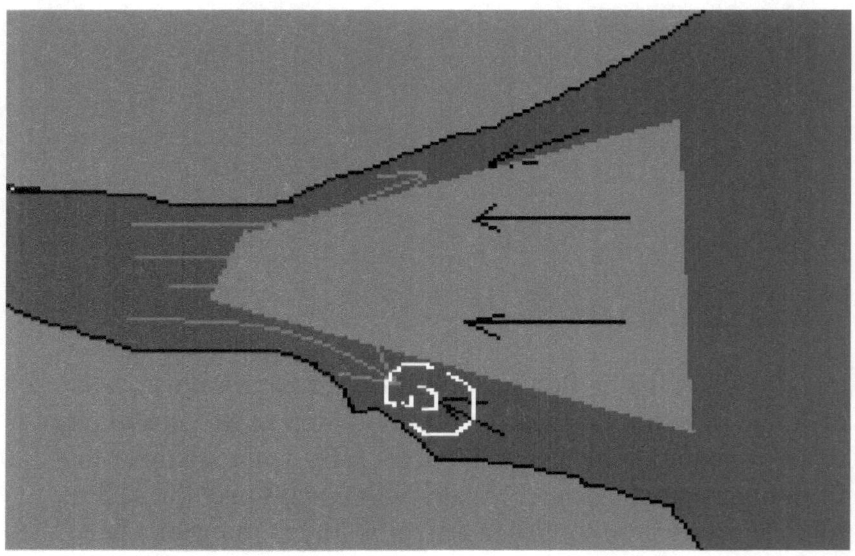

Just keep in mind fish are like lazy men, why work hard to find a meal? Find a spot where you can rest and have the meals come to you! Crap if I had said that at the beginning I could have saved myself a lot of time and trouble right? (Don't laugh, you know who you are!)

Well, now if finding fish is this easy, why don't more people catch more fish? I'd like to tell you a true story.

There's this place that I fished for years, I know most of the other fishermen, and they know me. One day a friend I've fished with for years asked me "What, gives with you and the fish around here?" I said "what do you mean?" He said "look I can almost set my watch by you. You get here every morning about 8:30 and the fish start biting almost right away? When you leave the fish stop biting. So what gives with you and the fish around here? Are the rest of us just, wakening the fish up for you to catch?" So I asked him "Well, what time do you get here?" he told me "about 4:30 am."

Disaster Survival!

Look, he's my friend so I tried not to laugh. Hell, even if he wasn't my friend I would have explained to him that, fish are like people and aren't hungry all the time. They eat, when they're hungry and in this spot they get hungry around 9:00am. Other parts of the river it could be earlier or later than 9:00am.

Every body of water is different, they all have their own time zones kind of. Once you know when the fish are biting on any body of water. Look at your watch because the fish will start to feed within about an hour either side of that time every day. This is also true for evening fishing.

The next morning when I drove up to the fishing spot, my friend was just getting there too! He told me that he would never again lose sleep fishing here ever again.

Usually if I go to a new lake or river I like to spend three days there. Day one will see me get up early so I can read/watch the water and do a little fishing. When I see the fish starting to feed I look at my watch to see the time. The next two days I will sleep until it's about an hour before the time I saw the fish feeding on the first day.

When the fishing slows down on any body of water, it's because the fish are full and have moved to deeper water to relax. At different times of the year the time it takes for a fish to get full varies. In the spring when the new hatch of minnows is small it takes a lot of these little guys to fill a big fish. So the fish might feed for over an hour or two. By midsummer the minnows have all grown up and it takes less of them to fill a big fish. It might take only a ½ hour to an hour for the big guys to get full.

You still have a chance to catch fish after they get full like some people some fish like a snack during the day. If you leave bait on a hook long enough, you'll probably catch one or two fish after the rest are full.

Okay, here's a tip if you fish with minnows take ½ a dozen tubes of mid to late summer minnow and keep them frozen till next spring. Hopefully your wife or girlfriend doesn't throw them out or eat them for sardines! Use them in the spring, and you should catch more and bigger fish with them.

The reason this works is that fish don't want to work hard for a meal. It's easier to eat one big minnow than four or five little ones.

Yes, I hear you; you said you don't bait fish! Let's see, you must be using jigs, plugs, spoons, spinners or flies or a combination of them. Well, you're in luck because so do I!

If I had to choose only one of the above mentioned tackle it would be the mighty jig!

So, why the jig, it's easy to carry a lot of them in a small box in my pocket. Don't believe me, a 4 inch by 6 inch box 2 inches deep can carry about 50 or so 1/8 ounce jigs. Add one more box the same size to carry about 80 or so rubber bodies of all colors and sizes for the jig heads and I'm good for about a 3 months of fishing!

Those two boxes of jigs and tails can be used in fresh water, salt water, muddy water, and clear water or any other water found worldwide. Not bad for about 1 pound or so of fishing gear that's without the rod!

I can hear the fly fisherman out there saying a fly rod can do all that and has the add advantage of using dry flies for surface fishing and the truth is their right! Using the same box mentioned above, it will hold about 100 or so subsurface streamer flies and another 50 or so surface dry flies.

The jig fisherman can cast live bail on a jig head which is next to impossible with a fly rod. So which rod is better?

I believe it's just personal preference. I love a fast action long cast spinning rod and reel, but don't ever ask me to give up using my sweet fast action 7/8 weight fly rod, because it's not going to happen! **Face it water, is water, and fish are fish, what rod you use to catch them is up to you!**

Besides, it's not the rod you use, it's how you shake it that counts! (You better be thinking about a fishing rod!)

Many years ago I learned this the hard way. There was a large group of us, fishing this river, but there was only one guy catching all the fish? What the hell was he doing the rest of us weren't? I got out of the river and sat on the bank and started watching this guy. My fishing buddy sat beside me and asked what I was doing. I told him that I was trying to figure out what that guy was doing to catch all the fish. We could see he was

using a spinning rod and a jig just like the rest of us. He was even using the same color rubber jig body as us so what gives?

What gives is that all the rest of us were casting out and reeling straight in. The guy we were watching wasn't. He was making the tip of his rod jump about 6 inches, reel in the slake jump 6 inches and reel in again, then make a 2 foot slide and then reel in the slack!

I went back into the river and started doing what he was doing and I started to catch fish! My fishing buddy came up to me and asked "what the hell are you doing now?" So I told him and he started to catch fish too.

We were the only three catching fish, no one else did and no one else asked me either. If they had asked I would have gladly told them what we were doing.

Just like reading water, it pays to read the guy, who's catching the fish when you're not. I also learned to change the way I reel in, sometimes fast, sometimes slow, maybe to the right, maybe to the left maybe up and down. Try and make your jig or whatever your using act more like a frightened or wounded minnow!

Jigs, plugs, spoons, spinners and streamer flies can all be used in fast or slow water. The idea is to cast passed there you think the fish might be (read the water) and reel in so the jig, plug, spoon, spinner or streamer flies passes within a foot of the target area.

In a river cast upriver and past a rock reeling in using the current to get within a foot or less of the rock. Be ready to set the hook as, your tackle passes the rock. If your fishing rapids cast above the rapids and let your tackle be washed down the river as you reel in. Always be ready to set the hook because a fish could strike at any time or place in the rapids.

If you're fishing the mouth of a river where it enters a lake or even the ocean cast up river and reel in as the current carries your tackle out into the slower water. The opposite is true if fishing where a lake empties into a river. Cast into the lake and let the current carry you're tackling down into the river. The idea is to have your tackle look like a wounded bait fish being swept along with the current.

In a lake, cast close to the weeds you can cast parallel to the weed line/mud line or perpendicular to them. Either way works and be ready for the fish to lunge out at your tackle. If you use weed less tackle you can cast right into the weeds. Sometimes you may see clear areas in the weeds. They may look like small trails or open patches cast into these as well.

If you're fishing a windy point of land cast into the wind the idea here is to use your tackle to initiate a fish coming from the windy side to the sheltered side of the point of land or a crippled fish drifting with the wind driven current... Fish will usually hit your tackle as it enters the windless protected area.

All the above works for spinning rods or fly rods with streamer flies! If you've never seen a wounded or frightened minnow and most of us never will. You can use or borrow a plastic, kiddies, swimming pool to see how Jigs, plugs, spoons, spinners and streamer flies react to the movement of your rod (just be sure the kids are out of the pool first!).

Bait fishing is done in slow to medium fast moving rivers or in lakes using a float or bobber about a foot or two above your hook and bait. The distance above the bait may and will change depending on how deep the water and/or the fish are so, play with the length if you don't get a bite. You let it drift till the float bobs up and down or dips below the surface of the water indicating a fish has bitten your bait. You may have to recast your bait from time to time while you wait. You can hold the rod while you wait or use a rod holder (a spring thing with a long, sharp end you push into the ground or a stick) so you can do other things. A rod holder is better than laying your rod on the ground, someone with big feet could step on it and break it or a fish could pull it into the water never to be seen by you again. Over the years I've caught three rods that others have lost, seen lots of broken ones and caught a six pack of beer! The beer must have fallen off a boat!

Another way to bait fish is to use a small weight (don't use a boat anchor!) ½ ounce is more than enough, if it's not the water is probably too fast for this kind of fishing. Use a walking weight and a single hook from shore or a pickerel rig you won't need a float/bobber as this is for longer casts from shore out into deeper water or dropping a line off a boat.

Dry fly fishing with a fly rod is a whole different animal. You cast a dry fly up river and let it drift on the surface of the river or lake. This method is used during a mayfly hatch or some other kind of water born insect hatch.

Chapter 5

Picking a Rod & Reel

Okay, now to pick a rod to fish with. Rods come in three actions fast, medium and slow actions. The action of a rod only means how much it will bend.

A slow action rod bends from the tip of the rod down to the hand grip. A medium rod bends from the tip of the rod down to about the middle of the rod. A fast action rod bends from the tip of the rod to about the first 6 to 14 inches of the rod.

Picking one action over another is a matter of personal preference. If this is your first rod or you don't have preferences yet, go to a fishing store and try out some rods.

For this exercise, don't look at the price of the rods you're not here to buy one your just trying to find a rod that feels good to you. Don't ask the salesperson to pick one for you, pick up one of each kind in turn and try some in store practice casting. Wave it around a little and see how it feels in your hand (don't fence with it or whip the salesperson or other customers!) Once you find a rod that feels good in your hand then that's the action for you.

Most rods are made with either fiberglass or graphite boron composite. Fiberglass rods will take a lot of hard use and are tough to break. However, they are not as sensitive when it comes to feeling a fish bite, but they are usually less expensive.

Graphite boron composite cost a little more and won't take the hard use like fiberglass. However, they are wonderfully sensitive and you'll feel the bite that would be missed on a fiberglass rod (again personal preference or your wallet will decide here!)

Rods also come in different lengths from about 5 feet to well over 10 feet. As a rule of thumb longer rods usually can cast a very lightweight lure. If you're looking for an average all round fishing rod, keep the length between 5 feet to 7 feet.

Rods also come in one piece or break down into two piece, three piece, and four pieces. Three or four piece rods are great for backpacking or canoe trips where you don't have much space. A two piece rod is great for the trunk of your car or the back of a pickup truck. A one piece rod is a little harder to store if you get one I suggest you spring for a rod case to keep it in or be real careful where you store it.

Most people get a two piece rod and you probably will too, but keep in mind where you will be storing it or what kind of fishing trips you're most likely to going on.

Okay, let's see you're, decided on the action you like, the length of the rod, the material the rod is made of and how many pieces it breaks down into. Now you need a reel for your rod.

The reels come in three basic types; spin cast/closed face, spinning reel/open face and bait caster.

Spin cast/closed face looks like it sounds; it's all closed in with only a hole for the line to come out in front. The front screws off so you can replace the line. This reel sits on top of the rod handle the rod and has a spur almost like a trigger of a gun on the underside.

Spinning reel/open face Again, it's like it sounds it has no cover over the line. The line is controlled by a wire bail and one finger, this reel hangs under the rod. This rod has no spur; the handle is straight with screw rings to hold the reel.

The bait caster is probably the oldest type of reel it looks like a very small towing winch you might see on the front of an all-terrain vehicle or a jeep. It also sits on top of the reel and would use the same kind of rod as the spin cast reel.

Disaster Survival!

All reels have a drag system, what this does, is to make it harder for the fish to take line off the reel. Set this to high the fish

can't take any line and the line may break. Set it to light, and the fish will be able to take all the line off the reel and you won't be able to slow him down. I set my drag by putting the hook into something solid and pulling the rod tip up.

If the line comes off too easily, then I increase the drag. What I'm looking for is a balance between letting the fish run and making him work for it without break my line. The thing to remember is to have your drag set about 2 to 4lbs lighter than your line.

So if you're fishing with a 10lb line try to set your drag at about 6 to 8 lbs. If the fish, is running, and taking line, don't try to reel him in, let it run.

If you reel in when he's taking line your line will start to twist on the reel and you will eventually end up with a large tangle of line on your reel. Hold your rod tip high this makes it harder for him to take the line. When he stops running lower your rod tip and reel in the line. Pull the rod back up and pull the fish towards you then as you lower the rod again reel in the line and continue doing this till he runs again or you land the fish.

Now that we know about rods and reels we need to put together a balanced rod reel combination!

Every rod has a line and weigh, limits and reads like this

(Line 4 – 10 lb lure 1/16 – ½ oz.) What this means it that the rod works best with line between 4 and 10lb test and a lure weigh between 1/16 and ½ ounces. You should never use a line or lure weights outside this range.

Reels also have limits and reads like this (line capacity yields. Lbs. 200 – 8, 170 – 10, 150 – 12). What this means it that the reel will hold 200 yards of 8lb test line and so on.

To get a rod and reel combination that is sensitive and casts great you have to have the numbers on the rod and reel that has the best match of line and weigh that you can get.

Snags, what are snags, how can we avoid them and still catch fish?

I would have never thought to write about snags because it's something we all have to live with if we're going to catch fish! Fish live in and around rocks, weeds, tree stumps, fallen trees and all kinds of underwater junk that cause snags!

One evening I was sitting with some friends having a few beers. I don't remember how the conversation got around to fishing, but it did. Amanda started telling me about fishing with her son and the snags they were getting, at their fishing spot.

No, I'm not going to give up your fishing spot Amanda! But a promise is a promise so here it is just for you!

OK, we've all had snags and have seen others get them. The best way to get out of a snag is from the opposite side of the snag. This will only work if you can cross said river or lake, a boat would be great! If you're fishing from shore, it's a good bet you don't have a boat handy.

Another way is to walk up or down the shoreline using steady pressure on your fishing line and hope it pops free. You can increase your chances of getting free by popping open the bail or pushing the casting button on your reel at different places on the shore line. The sudden release of the pressure on the line sometimes will kick your weight free. You can leave your tackle in the water and hope a fish takes your bait and helps free the snag.

As a last resort you can wrap the line around your hand and slowly pull the line increasing the pressure till it breaks. (Being careful not to cut your fingers off) The steady pressure will insure the line breaks close to the snag so you don't lose a lot of line that may end up snagging you or others later

The worst thing you can do is to wave your fishing rod around like your fencing with an invisible giant! Not only is this dangerous to others on the shoreline you're taking a chance of breaking your fishing rod. Also, your fishing line will most likely break at the tip of your fishing rod, leaving lots of line in the water for you to snag on later.

Most people I've talked to think that snags are caused by the hook getting caught on something. Well, most people would be wrong; it's the weight or sinker most of the time that gets hung up on rocks and stuff. I personally never use a weigh, heavier than 1/8 Oz and I get very few snags but I do get some.

Also, if you put your weight on lighter line, then your main fishing line using a barrel swivel the light line breaks first and you still might land the fish! (But you will still lose your weight)
Well, that's about it for now stop reading and go fishing!

WAIT the worst time to fish is on the weekends that's because everybody and their dog is out there boating, swimming, fishing and scaring the fish out into deeper water. If you can arrange it try fishing from Tuesday to Friday! Monday will still be slow fishing, do to all the traffic over the weekend.
(GOOD LUCK!)

What your back already?

Chapter 6

Different ways to catch fish

In a long term survival situation sport fishing won't keep you alive for long! There are hundreds of different ways to catch fish some legal others are not no so much. I'll try to get to as many of the good ways here or maybe not!

Check your local laws before you try anything written here! Don't break the law! If you do, don't get caught! If you get caught don't call me!   I've warned you!

Who were the first people to fish and how did they do it? I don't think anyone can answer that question with any certainty.
☺Fictional Story☺

Fishing probably got started when some caveman or other early hominid saw a bear slap or shove his head into the water and come out with a fish! So this hungry caveman/hominid figured that looks easy I'm going to give that a try! The first attempts to fish must have been funny to watch as it was dangerous to do. Here's some dude more, wild than tame jumping, divining, splashing and beating the water trying not to drown or get eaten by a bear and come up with a fish!

Don't laugh to hard this art of hand catching fish still exists today; it's called hand noodling, hogging, or feeling for fish. It's not for me, but down south people have turned it into a great sporting event to see who can get the biggest catfish by hand also other fish can also be caught this way.

Back at the old watering hole the caveman/hominid must have decided he needed some help and got a club or spear and some friends. By this time whole family groups have shown up, the guys trying to get the fish, the women and children on the shore watching and laughing at the men.

Well, it's always easier to see the player's mistakes from the sidelines so one of the women tried offering some help by saying there's too much water and started to explain what was needed to make catching the fish easier.

The guys by this time were tired, wet and humiliated and not in the mood to listen. Probably one said if you think you can do better then you try, I'm out of here. So he and the rest of the boys took off hunting/trapping.

☺Fictional Story Ends☺

For years fishing was the job for the woman and in some places around the world still is!

In the below picture you can see the solid black lines these are rock, that are piled on top of each other. The rocks are placed on top of each other so the water can flow through them, but are tight enough to stop the big fish from escaping. The light blue lines indicate the water flow. The three red arrows indicate the trappers walking up river and scaring the fish into the traps funnel. Once the fish are in the trap the trappers close the funnel with more rocks (the gray line over the mouth of the funnel). The red lines inside the trap shows, how the trappers push the fish into the shallow water. Once the fish are pushed into the shallow water they have to pass the trappers to get away and are much easier to club, spear, or grab. Even if the fish do get passed the trappers it's much easier to push them back into the shallows as it is harder for them to get out of the main trap. Just keep in mind to open the traps main blocking rock line at the top and bottom to let the fish up river when you're not trying to catch them.(can also be used at low tide for ocean fish by making a half moon from rocks)

Trap like this have been found that are 10,000's of thousands of years old. Also, traps of this size were used by large groups of people possible, as many as 5 or 6 families or a whole community would get together and trap fish. This trap can be designed to fit any rivers with a little modification.

Rock Trap

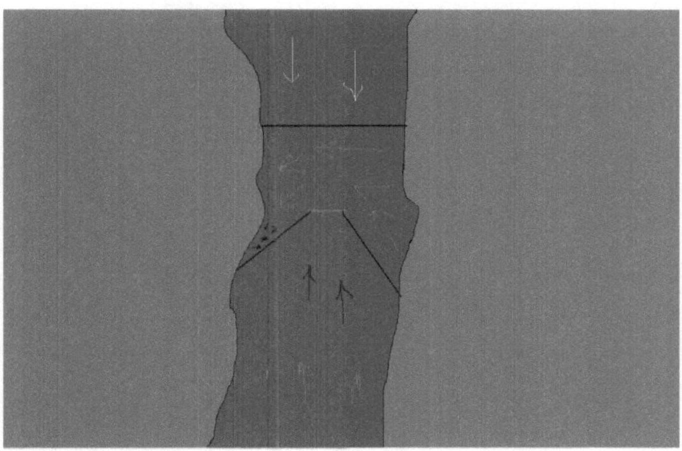

Some spear points Just take a stick make it pointy split the stick about 6 to 10 inches up and wedge a little stick into the split to keep it open. Now spear the fish across the back the little stick pops out and the slit closes up to hold the fish.

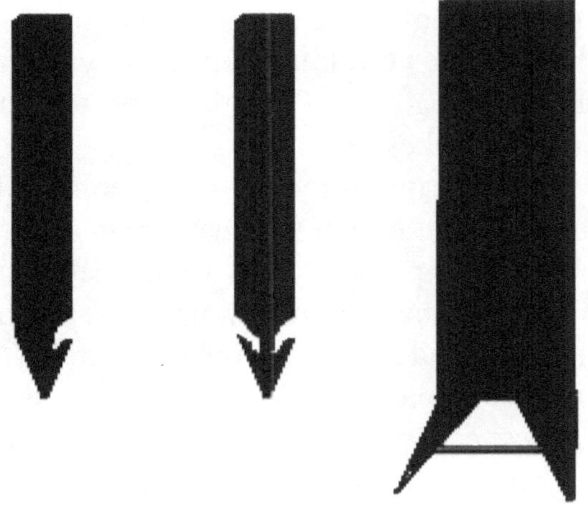

The above can be made out of the spokes from an old bike wheel. I've seen some gardening forks that if you took the handle off and put the head on a long stick it would make a great spear. Again, you have to use your imagination and you will find lots of ways to make a fishing spear. You do know that these will help you take frogs and snakes right.

So what if the river is too big and deep for this type of trap or maybe you want to trap fish that are, in a lake then what?

The M or W trap would work well. Keep in mind that you still have to use your ability to read water to trap fish. This is the easiest trap to make and the one I would rely on first if I was lost and hungry and had no tools with me! (No tools with me LOL not likely I always carry my Leatherman Wave multi tool knife with me!) Use sticks or rocks to make the letter M or W (it depends on the way you look at it). Don't make it too small about 3 feet across or bigger works well.

The M or W |Trap

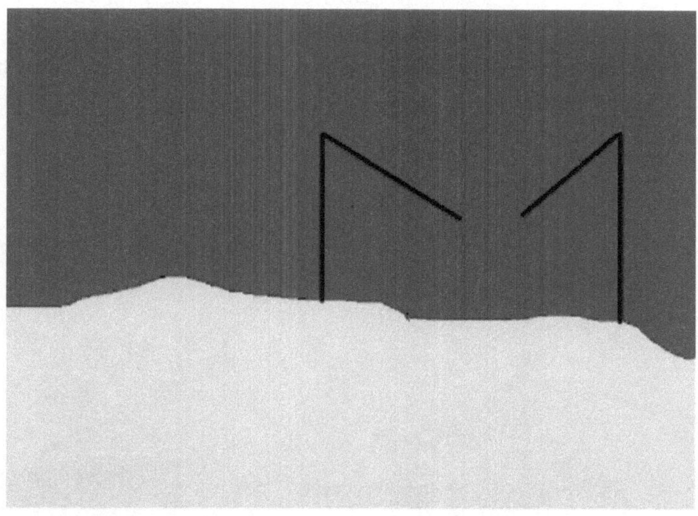

You'll have to use bait in this trap use anything fish will eat guts from other fish or animal works well, rotten fruit will sometimes work too. You can put the bait in the water or hang it above the water on a string tied to an overhanging branch or push a stick into the ground. If you're hanging it from a branch or a stick pushed into the ground, put it in a cloth or something what the flies can lay eggs on (this work with meat, fish guts etc. only). The eggs will turn into maggots and some will fall into the water and attract the fish. The fish, turtles and frogs will swim into the trap by way of the funnel in the M you can then club or spear them. All frogs in North America are editable, but you should always skin them first as some have poisonous skins, toads are not frogs learn to tell the difference and don't eat them! Turtles also make good eating. Be aware that if you are in an area where there are alligators this kind of hanging rotting bait may attract them too. Alligator hunters use this kind of hanging bait to catch them and it's where I got the idea from to use it for fishing! Your mind you your best survival tool so use it and think!

By the way, you can use the hanging bait without the trap and fish with a rod and reel using maggots, a small piece of popcorn, a small piece of white marshmallow or some other small bit of white on your hook and you can increase your

chances of catching fish. You can also tie a fishing line with hook and sinker to the stick just make sure the stick is deep in the ground so the fish can swim off with it.

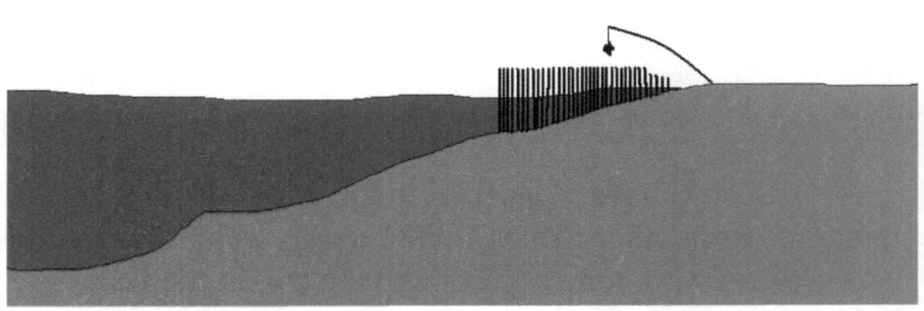

Okay, so you're on the move with a group of people and you don't want to spend time putting in traps. You can use a portable trap you can put in the water and later, take them out and carry them with you.

If the trap below looks like a minnow trap, then you're right. This type of trap can be made in all kinds of sizes from 1 foot long up to 3 feet and beyond and 1-2 foot in diameter. The red lines are cones with a large opening for the fish to swim in and a smaller opening on the inside to make it harder for the fish to get out then you pull the trap out of the water. The body of the trap is just a round tube or a square box made by weaving sticks together and tied with grass or string with the cones tied in at the ends. Put bait and stones in it to weigh it down and wait or go and do something else. You only need to check the trap once or twice a day to see if you caught a fish or two. Oh, it helps if you have a rope tied to it so you can pull it out of the lake, river or ocean. With different sizes of traps and water locations (fresh or saltwater) you can trap Fish, Crayfish, Lobster and Crab! For an ocean set the best times to put the trap in is at low, wide and/or wade/swim out in 10 or 20 feet from shore.

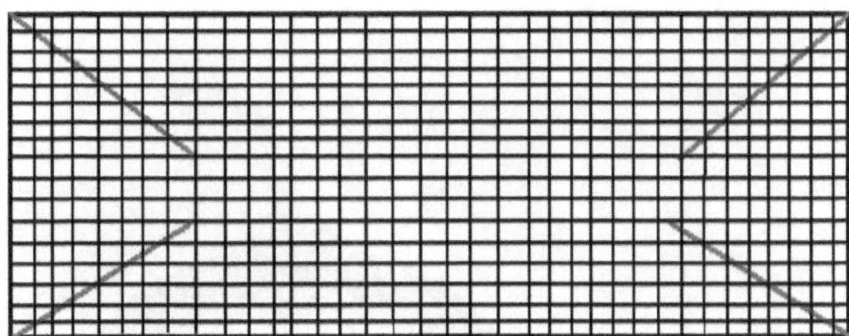

Yes a chain link fence would work just great, but don't use the neighbor's fence! A little wire from anywhere and you're set to go. If you think about it you can come up with lots of ways to construct traps of this kind. If you have a need to hide this trap you can hide the pull rope. Or don't use a rope at all, just throw it in the water and use a big hook (fishing gaff) on a stick, the head of a rake or anything that can hook the trap put it on a pole so you can reach the trap and pull it out. You could also leave a long pole near the trap and carry in the hook or rake head. This way is easier than carrying a rake or a pole through the woods.

Tire Trap

Old car tires without the rims can be turned into a fish trap. I was talking to a family friend about fishing; he was from Jamaica and told me this one! Lace or tie the side walls together with wire or strong rope. Cut two holes in the tread about three and a half to four inches big for the fish to swim in. The on the other side drill or cut one inch holes for the water to run out when you pull the tire out of the water, so it's not too heavy. You need to tie a rope around the tire right where you cut the holes for the fish to swim in. The idea is for the fish to swim down to the other end were the one inch holes are cut. Of course you will need bait in the tire, use fish guts or other animal parts for this.

The green arrows are where you cut the holes for the fish to swim in and the black line is the rope to pull the tire out of the water. The red arrows on the bottom are the drain holes for the water to run out. The yellow line is where you Lace tie, or sew the side walls together.

If you take a clear bottle, put some minnows in it, fill it water and put the cap back on, lower it over the side of your boat suspend it about two to three feet above the bottom of a lake you can attract fish. This makes it easier to catch them on a minnow baited hook.

Why Re-Invent the Wheel

A few years ago I found a small box full of gold! No not the kind you can sell on the gold market. It was a box full of old books! Most were Popular Mechanics so now I'll scan some items and past them here. It's my understanding that the copyright law has expired on them because they're so old, before the 1930's. Yes I have a copy of the copyright laws and it reads like ancient Greek!

Disaster Survival!

Picture below is from Popular Mechanics 1915

Homemade Glass Funnel

Look I know you think that this is in the wrong place, but
if you hang on a minute, you will see it's a good lead in for the
homemade glass minnow trap.

From Popular Mechanics 1913

An Emergency Glass Funnel

Secure a glass bottle having a small neck and tie a string saturated in kero-

sene around the outside at A and B as shown in the sketch. Light the string and allow it to burn until the glass is heated, then plunge the bottle quickly into water. The top or neck will then come off easily. The sharp edges are ground or filed off smooth. This will make a good emergency funnel which serves the purpose well for filling wide necked bottles.—

HOW TO MAKE A MINNOW TRAP

Popular Mechanics – 1913

Glass minnow traps that will give as good service as those purchased at the tackle store can be made without difficulty. If a trap should be banged carelessly against the side of the boat or some other obstruction and smashed, instead of spending several dollars to replace it, a half hour's time will turn out a new one just as good, says a correspondent of Outing.

A trap of this kind can be made from an ordinary fruit jar such as used in putting up preserves, either of one or two-quart capacity. A one-quart jar gives good results, but if the bait to be caught is of fairly large size, the two-quart size may be used. As the jars have the same style top they can be used interchangeably with one mouthpiece.

The mouthpiece is made of a round-neck bottle of which the glass is colorless and rather thin. If the neck of the bottle is cut at the right point, it makes a glass funnel that will just fit into the fruit jar. The funnel forms the mouth of the trap. Put the neck of the bottle into the fruit jar and mark the glass with a file where the bottle and jar meet. Make as deep a cut as possible with a file around the bottle on the mark and place two turns of a yarn string saturated in kerosene around just below the cut when the bottle is standing in an upright position. Set fire to the string and turn the bottle from side to side to distribute the heat evenly, then when the string has burned out, plunge the bottle in cold water and it will separate on the cut.

Bind some copper wire around the neck of the jar so that three ends will project $\frac{1}{2}$ in. or more. These are bent down over the funnel when put into the jar, forming clamps to hold it in place. The copper wire can be bent many times in emptying or baiting the trap without breaking.

Two copper wire bands are tied tightly around the jar about 3 in. apart. They should be twisted tight with a pair of pliers and the ends joined, forming a ring for attaching a cord.

For catching "kellies" or "killies," bait the trap with crushed clams or salt-water mussels and for fresh water shiners use mincemeat or bread crumbs and do not spill any bait outside of the trap. Leave the trap down ten to fifteen minutes and when resetting it after emptying, put back one or two of the victims, as the others enter more readily if they see some of their companions ahead of them.

Next, how to bait the trap to catch minnows you don't have to use bread or anything eatable this may also be used for other fish trap too. If you can attract minnows the big fist will follow them.

Popular Mechanics 1918

Catching Minnows for Bait

Instead of chasing the little fish up and down the stream to catch enough for bait, try putting a clean bit of shell in a wide-mouth jar and holding it in the water. The minnows will be attracted in great numbers, and it is an easy matter to dip them up. A bit of shell can be used also in a net. The white, shining shell seems to be a good lure for the little fellows.

You don't have to hold it you can tie a rope to it and quickly pull it up that way.

Long line/trot line

A Long line/trot line is just that a long rope with drop lines on it and anchored at both ends No it doesn't use boat anchors but it could. It's easier to tie one end to the shore (tree etc.) the other end, to a rock. Throw, wade, swim, boat or use a log to get out into deeper water and drop the rock. The drop lines have weights and hooks on the ends just like a fishing line with bait, easy right!

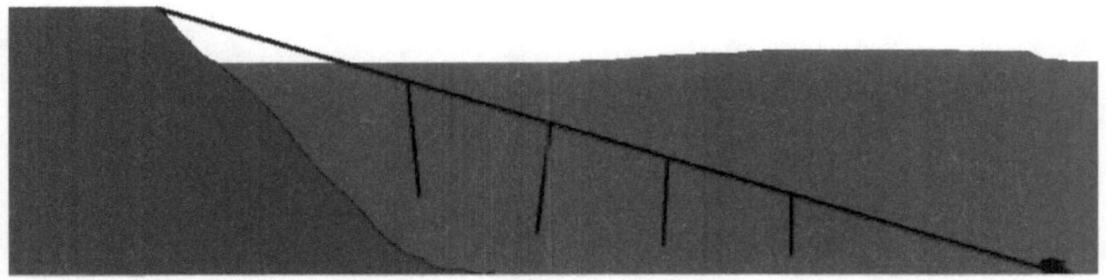

The top picture could be set in a river, lake or the ocean! The next set below could be used between two points of land in a lake/ocean bay or narrow river.

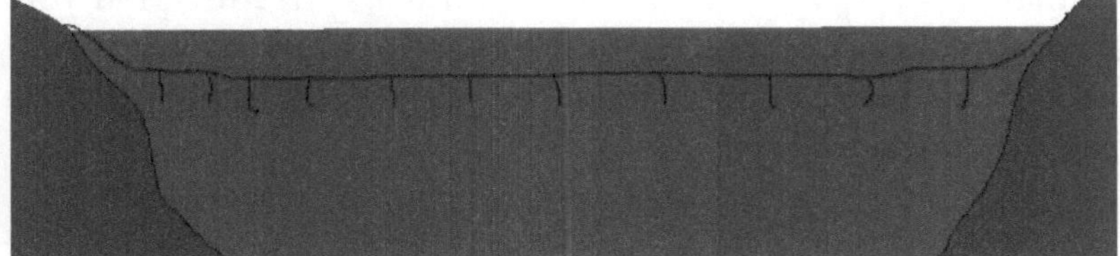

No bay, well, get out into the water as far as you can at low tide and try putting two poles deep into the mud tie your line to it and hang your drop lines on it.

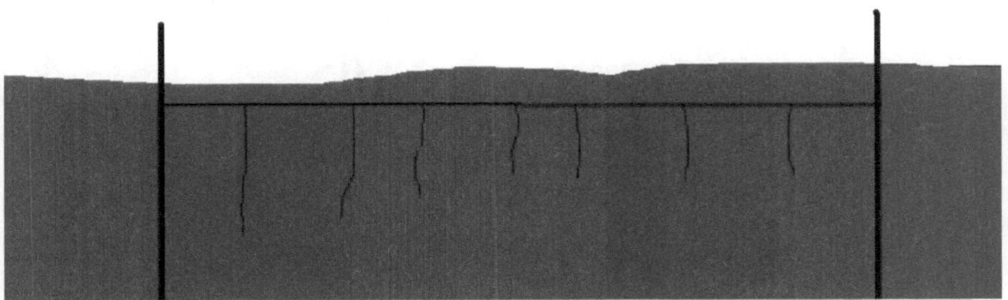

Home Made Hooks

If you don't have hooks or you don't have enough use a small stick about ½ - 1 inch long tie your line in the middle of the stick. Impale your bait on the stick so the fish will swallow the bait and stick. The stick will get stuck in its gut and you can pull it in. You've probably caught fish that have swallowed your fish hook before well this is the same idea.

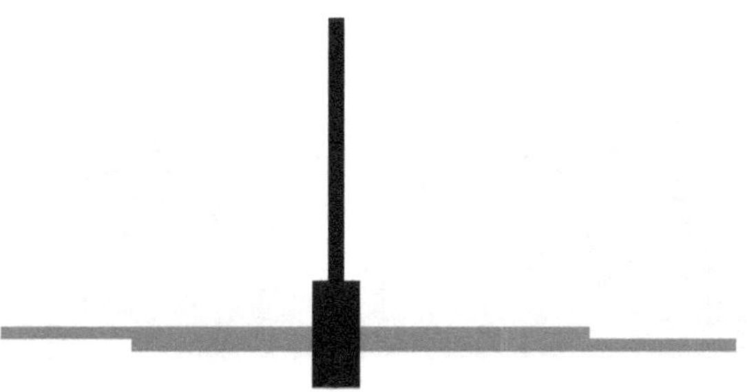

You used to get small clear glass bottles from the drug store. I don't know if you still can today or not. However, you can get small clear liquor bottles that would work, like the kind you get on airplanes. Like the big bottles put your bait in them tie hooks on the bottle and use them for bait fishing, the bait can be small minnows or bugs

Picture below is from Popular Mechanics 1915

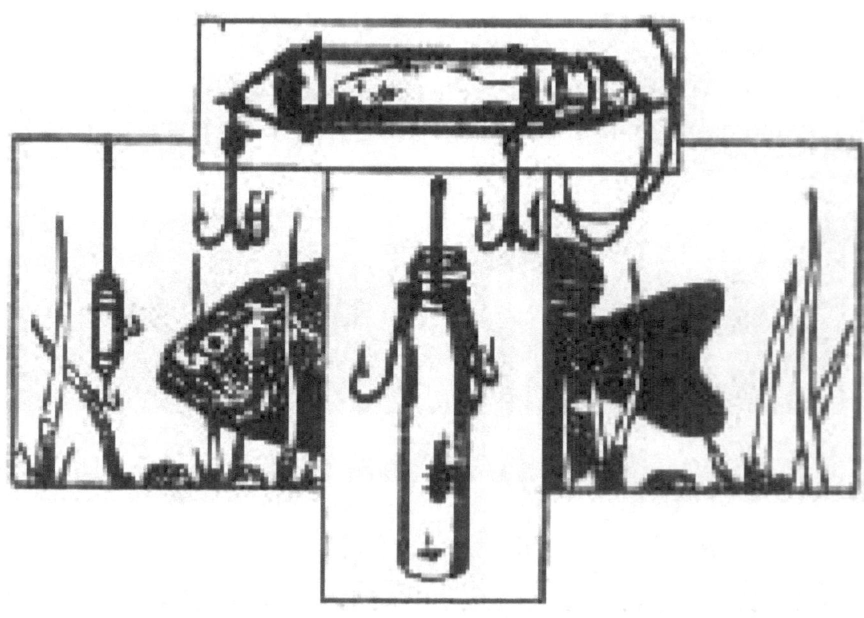

Picture below is from Popular Mechanics 1919

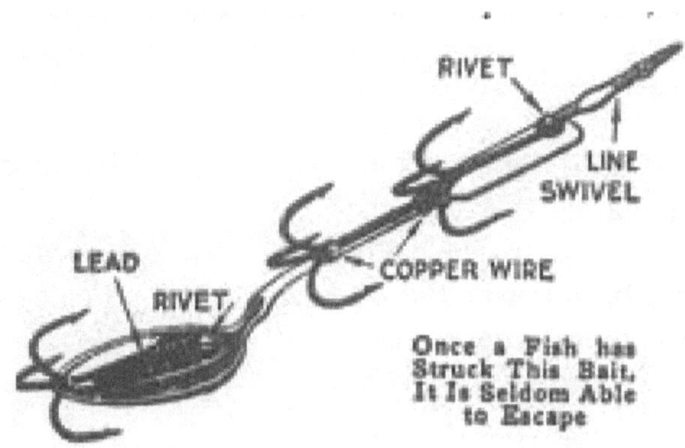

Bobber fishing with a twist!

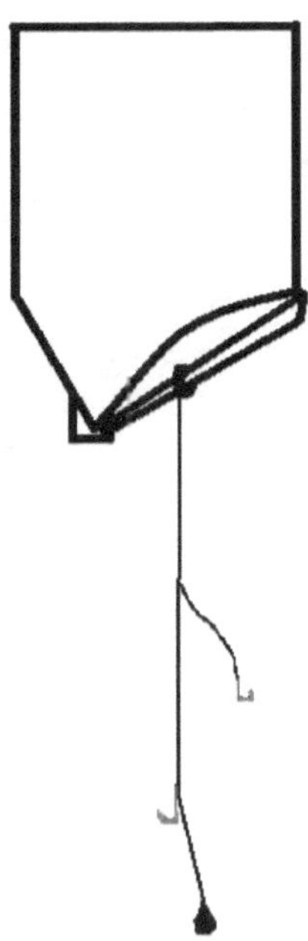

Any old plastic jug without holes in it will work.
However, jugs with handles work best because you can tie your
fishing line to the handle. A good 8 or 10 feet of line will work.
Oh, if you haven't figured it out yet you're going to need a boat!

Well, anything that you can paddle in a small lake or pond. Why a small lake or pond? Well the fish are going to drag this rig all

over the lake. If the lake is the size of Lake Eire good luck trying to find it again!

So you don't have a boat well fear not because fortunately the people back before the world got so complicated and crowded knew how to improvise.

HOW TO MAKE A BARREL BOAT

Popular Mechanics – 1915

A boat that any handy boy can easily make is constructed of a barrel which is kept with the opening cut in one side up by two 4 by 6-in. timbers and two tie pieces, 2 by 4 in. The lengths of these pieces will depend on the size of the barrel.

A good watertight barrel should be selected and an opening cut in the center between the hoops, of such a size as to allow the body of the occupant room for handling an oar. The timbers are attached to the barrel with iron straps—pieces of old hoops will do. The two tie pieces are put across the timbers at the ends of the barrel and spiked in place.

The boat is to be propelled with a single, double-end paddle. There is no danger of the boat capsizing or the water splashing into the barrel.

Boat Made of a Barrel Which Is Kept from Capsizing by Timbers Attached

Making a Catamaran Raft
From Popular Mechanics 1925

A simple raft, that will meet the requirements for an inexpensive and simple

A Useful Boat, Built of Logs as a Catamaran Raft,
Takes the Place of a Regulation Rowboat When
the Latter is Not Easily Obtained

boat, can be made from two or three logs in the manner indicated in the drawing.

Two logs, about 12 ft. long, are used for the sides, and connected with crosspieces, spikes or wooden pegs being used to secure the parts together. A piece of split log answers for a seat, and two forked branches, inserted into the sidepieces, make satisfactory oarlocks. In the absence of regulation oars, pieces of board can be cut to approximately the proper shape.

While you're out and about watch out for turtles, frogs and snakes especial snakes, some have deadly poisonous bites and will kill you if you get bitten but they're all good to eat!

All frogs have to be skinned before you cook and eat them because some have poisonous skin, so never eat the frog skins! Roast, fry, or throw them in a stew pot. After cleaning and cutting them up first!

All snakes are eatable, nonpoisonous snakes are (said?) to have round pupils in its eyes, poisonous snakes are (said?) to have oval shaped pupils in its eyes. I don't know if this is true, I've never seen a poisonous snake. However, if you are close enough to see its pupils your to dam close! No, I'm not joking this time, but you could be choking and dying! If you kill one cut off the head about an inch or two down past its head, gut it and then eat. You can cook them just like you would with the frogs.

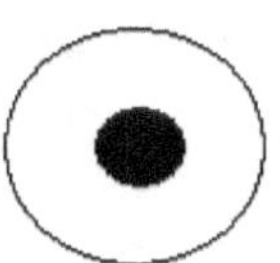 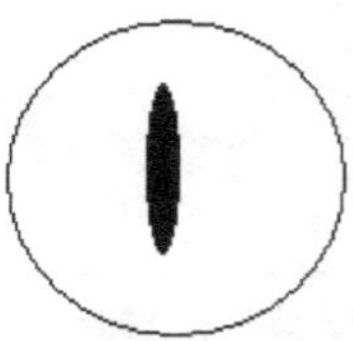

Fishing nets

When I was living in Newfoundland I help my friend and his dad with his commercial fishing nets and lobster fishing. We were fishing for Cod with a one hundred and fifty foot net I think it was. No you don't need a net this big. We were using his net anchored from the shore the other end was anchored one hundred and fifty feet out in the bay. Look back at the trot line setups and you'll know what I'm talking about!

The main difference between a net and a trot line set is that the net has floats, about every three feet along the top and weights about every three feet on the bottom.

Disaster Survival!

Your mind is your best survival tool and back then they really know how to think! It seems that now in this age of factory made everything we stopped using our minds to improvise thing we need.

Okay, you live in a city hundreds of miles away from the ocean where do you find fishing nets? Well, look around is there any commercial lake fishing in your area? Still no!

All is not lost! If you've been paying attention up till now you might know where to find nets! Survival is not about having everything you need, stored up for the big disaster! It sure helps if you do, but we are not all rich right? Again, remember, your mind is your best survival tool so use it!

Survival is all about knowing where to find the things you need and make or improvise things you can't find! Again! Survival is a mindset you can have all the survival gear you want, but if you don't have the will to survive it probably won't do you any good! You should also know how to use it you gear, fix it, find replacement parts or how to improvise parts or stuff you don't have!

Okay, crunch time did any of you think of a sporting goods store?

Volley Ball Nets! Badminton Nets! Tennis Net! Soccer Nets! Hockey Nets! Basket Ball Hoop Nets!

YES, you can catch fish in these nets and the Basket Ball net, works GREAT for the ends of the fish trap made with the chain link fence! You can also put a handle on it to make a landing net/dip net. You will have to close the little hole so the fish don't swim out of it. If you're on the coast you could use it in a crab or lobster trap!
If you're going to use a big net (Volley Ball Nets, Badminton Nets, Tennis Net, or Soccer Nets) you're going to have to place weights on the bottom of the nets (any scrap metal about a half pound or so will do) and floats (plastic bottles will work) on top. These nets would be used with one end anchored to the shore and

the other end offshore in a river/lake/ocean. I don't have to tell you you're going to need a boat/canoe or something that floats at least, do I? Well, that's not actually always true! If you're by the ocean you might find a spot where you can set up the net at low tide so you don't need a boat. Just look back at the long line/trot line for ideas on how to use these big nets.
However floats on the top of the net are not always needed.

If you place a net across a river you might like the boats to go over the net without hitting or seeing it. Without floats the net will need to be tied off on both sides of the river by leaving slack in the main tie off line you can have the top of the net as deep or as shallow under the water as you like.

Nets like all traps need to be checked twice a day, once in the morning and again that evening. **Never leave a net or trap set up in the wild** when you have enough food take the nets or traps home again!

I can hear you! You said I'm not going to buy an expensive Volley Ball Net, Badminton Net, Tennis Net, or Soccer Nets just to throw it into the water! Well, you can make a net, it's not too hard, but it will take a half a day or more depending on how big you make it. In the picture the top black line is really a yellow nylon rope, but it doesn't have to be. You could use an old close line, the kind that has the plastic outer cover or just the bare wire or almost anything else, use your imagination and think!

The red and green drop lines are 15 to 20 pound test braided Dacron fishing line. No you don't have to use just the Dacron line again use your imagination the twine the butcher uses to tie up your meat will work too. I use red and green in the picture to show how the net is tied. The line comes in basic black. The top line will determine the length of the net and the drop line the depth of the net.

Hang your main line between two objects then tie on your drop line in even numbers 2, 4, 6, 8 who do we appreciate etc. The distance between the drop lines will determine the size of the holes when the net is finished. The holes in the net can be from

1½ to about 4½ inches apart. The small holes will take fish like pan sized fish larger holes for lake trout or anything in between.

Take the first, red and first green drop lines and tie them together. Then take the second red and green drop lines and do the same. Try to keep the knots all lined up use a ruler or a board as a spacer, just keep them lined up. Keep tying the lines till you're at the end of the main line. Once you reach the end start the second row by taking the first green line using your ruler or board to keep the same space and tie it to the second red drop line. The third row will be the first red and the first green drop line again, keep this pattern up row after row till the net is as big as you want it to be.

If you started with a 10 foot main line and your drop lines were 7 feet long you'd end up with a nice net for fishing small rivers, ponds and bays in larger lakes.

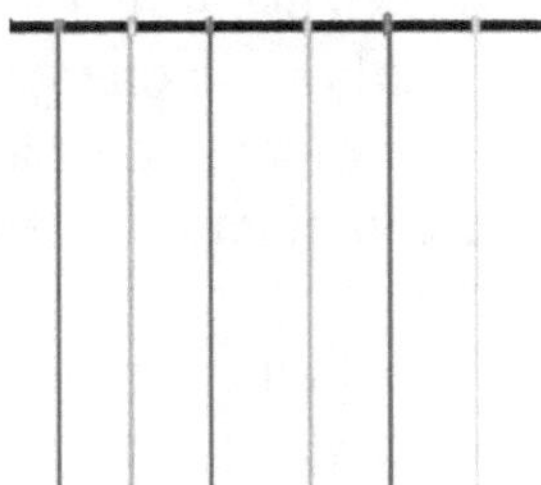 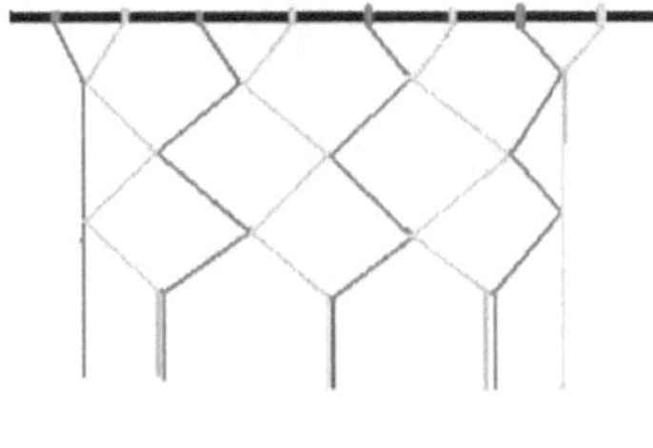

I remember my friend's dad saying he caught ducks in his net from time to time. He had his net placed near a small cove in the spring so it might be a way to catch some ducks if you can find the right place. I talked to other shore fishermen and they tell the same story about catching ducks from time to time. If you put your net where the ducks like to feed and use some bait then your chances of catching ducks just got a whole lot better. Oh, if you're a bad boy/girl and are poaching don't use corn or other color baits always use green it harder for the law to see it. This is true with all baits for any game birds!

James Evans Sr.

Black Walnuts

No, black walnuts are not the ones you eat at Christmas or buy in the stores. Black walnut trees grow wild in North America and the natives use the outer green husk of the nut to poison fish. The inner nut is good for people to eat and the poison husk is only poisonous to cold blooded animals, fish and insects.

I first heard about black walnuts when I was in Southern Ontario were some trees still grow wild there, but some are used for ornamental shade trees.

I was told that in the fall when the nuts are still green and on the trees. The Natives would harvest some of them and scrap the outer husk, off the nuts. The husks were then pounded into a paste and the paste was spread over a small area in a river there the fish were. After a little time fish would be seen swimming around near the top of the water and could be caught by hand or speared. The husks float so if you're going to use it in a lake you'll need to put it in something. I was told to use one gallon milk or juice container drop two or more of them in a small bay and wait. You'll have to put rocks in the containers to make it sink to the bottom.

Now, there's some confusion as to whether or not the fish were just stunned or if this would kill them. Years later I found out that this poison will definitely *kill* the fish! It seems that the active poison in the black walnut husks is retention, which is used in pesticides. The Rotenone coats the gills of the fish and they can't get oxygen from the water and the fish suffocate and die!

A long time ago and maybe still today, conservation officers used Rotenone to kill all the fish in lakes trying to kill off all the snakehead fish. Not to worry the lakes were restocked with more desirable fish.

So if you can't find black walnuts look in the commercial plant nurseries and get the highest percentage of Rotenone you can find. The lower the percentage the more you'll have to use to get the job done. Start out with small doses till you find what works well for each percentage.

The pesticides come in liquid and powder, mix the liquid with flower and the power with water.

There are other plants the natives use to fish with and here's a list of some.

Horse Chestnut, use the Fruit and buds
Polk Sallet, Polk weed, use the Berries
Turkey-Mullein, use the Leaves
California Buckeye, use the Nut or fruit
Soap plant, soap root, use the bulb
Indian hemp, use the Stalk, leaves
Indian turnip use the Leaves
Wild cucumber, **Man root,** use the Seeds

Do I need to remind you to make a paste out of the plants, leaves, and seeds etc.? Have a look in your area when you're out and about you just might find some of these plants.

Electric Generator

Believe me, I know how it sounds! However, I was watching a documentary about Asian (jumping, silver) carp in American waterways. The conservation officers were using an electric generator in their boat to stun the fish and count them.

Sorry I didn't see what kind of generator or what wattage they were using. I think if one was using the generator producing 1000 watts of 110ac currant that should do the trick. Cut off the female end of an extension cord. Attach a metal rod to one lead and hang it over the side, front or back of your boat. The other lead will need a rubber handle and a long metal rod. This lead is for you to hang onto and probe the water with.

All you have to do now is plug in the modified extension cord start the generator and fish with it.

With the conservation officers using this method, it would be a dead giveaway if you're seen putting a generator in your small rowboat.

However, if you get yourself a deep cycle marine battery you won't look so suspicious. You will also need a power inverter one that will, produce 1000 watts of 110ac currant. Hook the battery to the inverter and plug in your modified extension cord and go fishing. Your mind is your best survival tool so use it **Just stay out of the water and don't zap any swimmers!**

No, I didn't forget about fishing with explosives! I just think that there are too many ways for your kids to get hurt and I don't want that to fall on me!

The thing is I was trained in how to use explosives, when I worked underground in the mines up in northern Ontario. So trust me about this one you don't need to use them to survive!

The truth is if I had to do it over again, I would have spent more time on learning about eatable plants that can be found in the city or out in the country side growing wild and less about explosives.

Chapter 7

Hunting VS: Trapping

This will be a short introduction about hunting, as there are so many books out there right now that I think you should read them. This way I don't have to re-invent the wheel. I'll just cover what I think are the big three for survival hunting, deer, moose, and bear.

Anyone that has gone hunting guys or girls knows that it's fun to be out and about in the country. You spend all day, maybe you get something, maybe not, but you never feel that the day was wasted because you had fun. Your hunting for food and you may even feel you're the biggest predator out there carrying a rifle.

So how many ways are there to hunt do you just walk around and hope to see something to shoot and bring it home to eat? Do you find a place to sit and wait, how do you even know where the game is or how to find them? If you've never hunted before, what do you do? Well, most will go hunting with someone that knows how or as at least has hunted before.

Let's play a game of what if. What if you've never hunted before, what if you don't know anyone who has hunted before, what if none of your friends are interested in hunting. What if you have from childhood always wanted to be a good hunter and outdoors men that can you do?

You just turn 18 or 16 depending on the laws in your area. You have a good job and you decide this is it I'm going to go hunting this fall no matter what! You complete the entire legal requirements to buy the rifle or shotgun of your dreams and you get your first deer hunting license.

Remember the triangle of life I spoke of before? All animals need water, food and a safe place to sleep. That's where you start to get all the information you need, then you study, study, and study some more.

Find hunting books, magazines, videos, and movie documentaries about the animal you're going to hunt. Knowing when, where, and how to find them you need to get your maps in order. It took me one whole winter of studying deer to learn about them before I ever went hunting for them. You see, in Newfoundland we don't have deer, to hunt, but I wanted to try hunting deer and wanted to be prepared.

My first deer hunt was rather disappointing for me. I went hunting with a group of six hunters that had hunted the area we were going to before. One of them asked if I had hunted deer before and I told him "No, never." (BTY at the time I was working on a farm in rural Manitoba)

The first day I had to push the bush with two other guys so the deer moved out in front of us. The other three guys were what they called the standers, they would shoot any deer that came out of the bush that try to get away from us. This kind of hunting is called driving and works well if you have others that will go hunting with you.

On day two it was the drivers turn to be the standers and we would get a chance to shoot our deer. I could hear movement in the bush coming towards me and then saw the deer. I raised my rifle and took aim the deer stop and disappeared!

Like most I've seen lots of deer standing in open fields, but I never saw one disappear before? I just can believe that just happened was I dreaming? I raised my head a little and squinting, my eyes YES the deer was still there.

About 30 feet inside the brush line standing almost side-on to me. I readjusted my aim, fired and the deer went down and disappeared again! I was not dreaming deer have the best camouflage I have ever seen when they stop moving in the bush!

It was nice to be out and about and to get some wild meat, but all in all this was not hard at all to do. Other than the fact deer are hard to see if standing in a little bit of cover. So why do so many hunters say deer hunting is such a big challenge It's because they don't know anything about how the deer lives.

LOL remember the guy that asked if I had ever hunted deer before. Well, later that day he said to me "You said you never hunted before?" I told him no, you asked if I ever hunted deer before and I hadn't. I've hunted Moose, Bear and Caribou but never I never hunted deer. He and the other guys had a bet that I would get buck fever and not be able to shoot a deer.

So how is this done? The three standers pick their spot to stand the drivers line up at the other side of the bush. They walk slowly so they don't start the deer moving too fast and they keep walking till that exist the bush on the other side close to the standers.

Black squares the standers, the red lines the drivers, the green is the bush, and the yellow is the field.

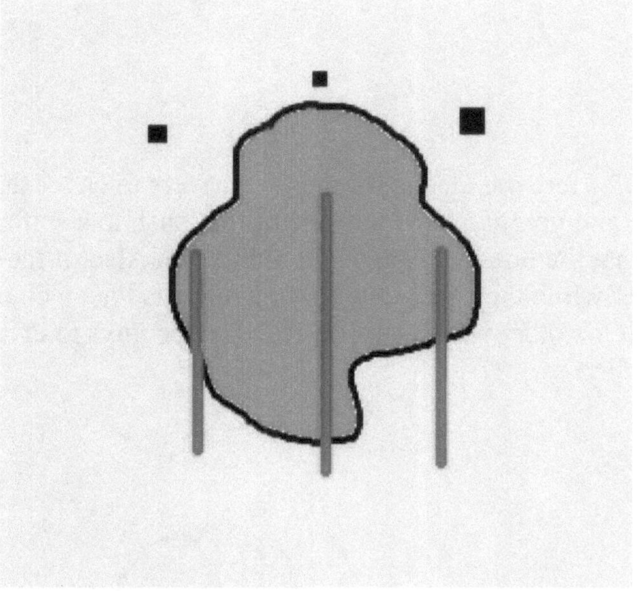

The same bush can be hunted with just three guys.

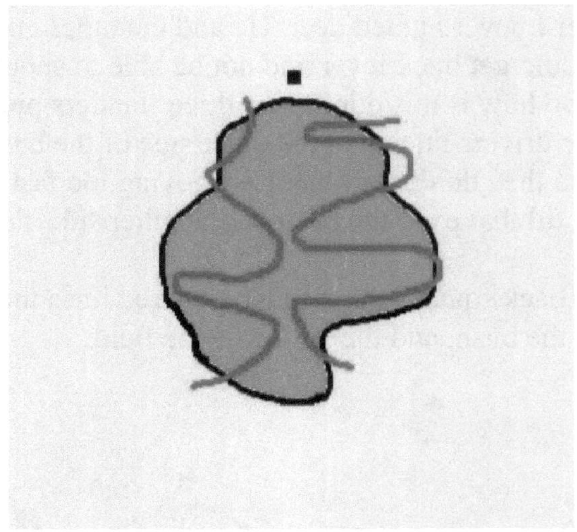

Here the idea is for the two drivers to cover the entire bush and going out at each side of the, bush to see if any deer got out that the one lone stander couldn't see. Also, if the drivers see a deer while they are walking they may also get a chance to shoot one. One other way would be for all three guys to drive the deer together.

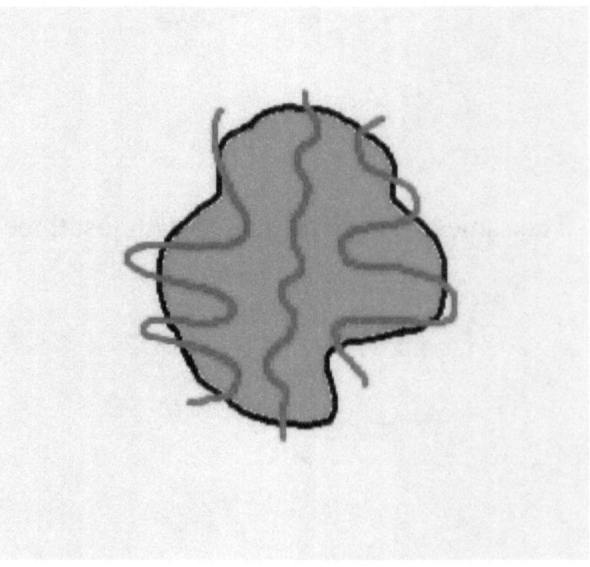

Two guys could drive the deer, but it's much harder to do successfully.

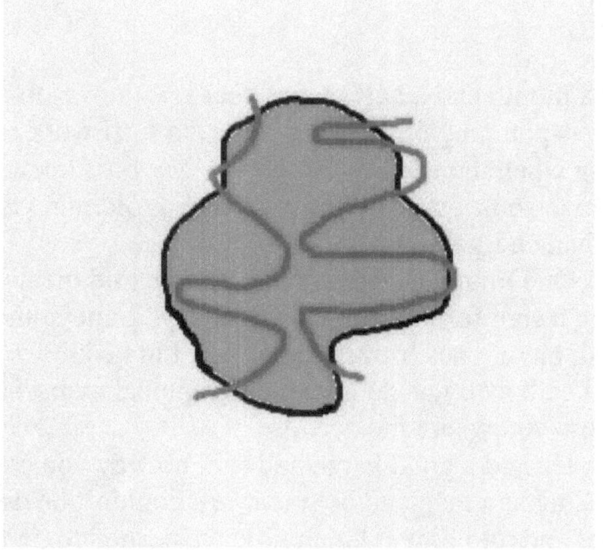

I never liked this way of hunting, especially if you have guys that have never hunted before or are still learning how to hunt. It's way too easy for a new and nerves hunter to shoot at and maybe hit one of the other guys! It may also explain why there are so many hunting accidents when deer hunting.

Always and I mean always have a clear sight of your target before squeezing the trigger! Never ever combine drugs or alcohol with or before hunting, if you do, you're just asking for a tragic accident to happen!

This type of driving deer plays on the fact deer like to eat at dusk, dawn and under cover of night. Deer will sleep and rest during the day and if you know there they sleep you can drive them out into the open!

Another method of hunting Deer is still hunting. This method is all about knowing there the deer go to feed, drink, and where they sleep. This is about ambushing them as they move from one area to another. You're going to have to do some field work during the day to find a good spot to ambush them from.

This reminds me of another true story that happened to me when I was working in the city of Winnipeg Manitoba. It was

about a month and a half before deer season was to open. My boss was planning on booking three days off work and go deer hunting when the season opened. .   My boss knew I was an avid fisherman so he asked if I ever hunted. I told him yes, but hadn't hunted since I got to the city.

One thing leads to another and he told me he had been hunting a spot for three years and always came home empty handed, having never even see a deer, but he knows the deer were there. I said well lets go get a topographical map of the area and I'll show you where the deer are.

He had a good laugh and said no way you can find deer by looking at a map and bet me it just couldn't be done! I took that bet and told him at lunch time we needed to go to Manitoba Conservation 1007 Century Street because it's where I get all my fishing/hunting maps from.

BTY every city and most small towns have a place like this and you can find them in the phone book. When this story took place the internet was not in every home like it is today. You can ask the sales person for the maps or look up the maps for yourself.

I asked my boss for the nearest town to where he hunted I looked in the index book found the name and the corresponding map number. He paid for the map and back to work we went, it was just that quick and easy.

A topographical map is about 3x3 feet square and the town you ask for or look up will be close to the center of the map. These maps show every little detail of the ground around the town or city. Everything like lakes, marshes, farmland, gravel pits, mines, and wooded areas I mean everything is there to see.

I asked him to show me where he was hunting and he pointed to a spot on the map. Now this spot was a heavily wooded area with a small lake. I told him that, that area looked more like moose country. He frowned and gave me a sideways look and said I seen a guy back there last year and he said he had just seen a moose.

I pointed to a large gravel pit and said that's where the deer are right there. We both agreed we would get together after the first snowfall and go have a look at this gravel pit to see who was right and who would win the bet.

Yes, I won the bet that the gravel pit was full of deer tracks. The second day of the deer season my boss comes in and I asked him what are you doing here? You had three days off didn't you? He didn't even look at me when he said that was just too easy.

He told he had gotten there about an hour or so before sunup got into position and about an hour after sunup he saw the deer he wanted, one shot one kill, and he was home before lunch.

So why did this work out to be so easy? Remember the triangle of life water, food, and a safe place to sleep. This works because I know what the deer want to eat and where they will most likely find the food they want. Deer also will behave in the same manner in the evening so both times can be very productive.

For the most part moose like a heavily wooded area to feel safe with some marshland and or lakes nearby. Finding a spot to wait for a moose to come to you is probably the best way to hunt them in my opinion. Use a tree stand or any other, form of cover close to the trail leading to water, where they come to drink and feed.

Why marshland and wooded lakes because moose love water plants and underwater vegetation to eat. Also the marshlands and lakes will attract migratory ducks and geese. The lakes will most likely have fish, frogs, turtles, snakes and maybe crayfish. If this sounds like an all you can catch food buffet then you're right.

BTY male moose in the fall mating rut are very dangerous, much more than any bear and very unpredictable. You may have heard about moose chasing hunters up trees and other wild stories; you had better believe them because most of them have happened!

Deer on the other hand, are low browsers and nibble on low plants and shrubs. Gravel pits working or abandoned have

everything a deer could want. I have never seen a gravel pit in deer country that didn't support a large number of deer. Here you will also find upland game birds, rabbits and other small game animals and maybe bears.

What if you don't have gravel pits in your area, farm fields or any or open grassland with small islands of wooded areas is a good bet as well. Deer also like lakes near gravel pits and open field as well as farmer's dugout and cattle watering holes. You can find them in apple orchards even a single apple tree will attract them and in the spring the salt licks that the cattle ranchers put out for the cattle will attract them.

This account may seem too easy and for the most part it was, everything worked out very well for him that day. Just don't expect it to happen day after day because it won't. Deer are smart and will learn and become very wary because the pressure of hunting them in the same area day after day they may start to feed at different times of the day. They may wait till full dark to come out or even move to a less desirable place to feed. I should mention that the wind direction, is important here always have the wind blowing in your face while you're looking toward the area where you think the deer will enter the clearing from.

Bears, well bears are omnivorous; all, this means is they will eat any food they come across. With a few exceptions bears are loners and they roam around looking for food item. The exceptions are they are attracted, to garbage dumps. Always again **always** in bear country, keep your garbage well away from your camp and your food hung up in trees away from your campsite as well. The other exception is if you live on the coast where you have a salmon run. These salmon runs attract larger number of bears.

How do you find signs of bears in the country? Well the easiest ways is if you see one, if you didn't see you then it becomes harder. Start by looking for bear tracks in the soft ground near water or along dirt roads. Look for old fallen trees that have been ripped apart, bears do this looking for bugs and grubs. Bears like to use the same tree year after year to scratch and rub against. These trees will have unusually smooth patches of bark and broken branches on them. Last you can look for trees with claw marks on them, bear mark trees this way to show that he was there and show how big and powerful he is to other bears coming into this area.

The best way to shoot a bear is to have him come to you; you will need to use bait, lots of stinky rotten food/garbage meat once you find signs of bears in the area.

Traps

If hunting can be so productive why trap? Well, if you're on your own or there are just a few people then trapping will be important. Hunting will, by its nature will not always be productive. There will be lots of days hunting that you won't get anything at all. There will also be days where you have too many things to do around your campsite.

If you have traps for small game within 10 to 15 minutes from your campsite you will not have to spend half the day hunting. If you have lots of people have your best hunter take a different person each day with him, so everyone gets a day of hunting, checking traps and some much needed practice. It also helps with morale and breaks up the tedious routine and if your best hunter gets hurt or sick you have other trained people on hand.

This will be another short introduction to trapping in a disaster/pandemic with no budget for all the goodies that other may have what do you do?

A trap is only as good as the trigger you use; the trigger has to work first time every time! Well, some traps don't use triggers!

Traps for small game works better than hunting them with a rifle or handgun, because traps don't use bullets and you don't have to be there for them to work. It's like having someone out there all the time and all you have to do is check the traps every morning and evening. If the traps are within 10 to 15 minutes from your campsite you lose very little time and more work gets done around your campsite.

There are four kinds of traps they ether strangle, tangle, dangle, and mangle. However, some will strangle and dangle.

Snares: strangle
Nets: tangle, and baited fish hooks with a line tied to a branch/stick/plastic bottle.
Snares: can strangle and dangle with the use of a springy sapling
Mangle: figure 4 dead falls, the jaw traps.

If the jig is the best all-around winner for fishing, then the snare would be the best all-round winner for trapping. With the snare you can take everything from a mouse to an elephant and in some cases you can use it to catch fish. The average snare is light and it's easy to carry 12 to 24 in your shirt pocket.

So, let's have another reality check in a disaster even if you have canned food you still should be trying to catch small game, because it will make the canned foods last longer. Also, we will not try to trap mice or elephants and other very large animals. We will be after rabbits, squirrels, house cats, and other animals of the same size.

Snares for small game can be made out of any fixable wire like brass, copper, picture wire, and even your shoe lace or other strong string. If a picture is worth a thousand words, then I just save myself lots of typing.

I'll start with a computer USB cord which would not be my first choice just like I would have to be desperate to use my shoelaces for a snare.

Start by cutting the ends off, the USB cord.

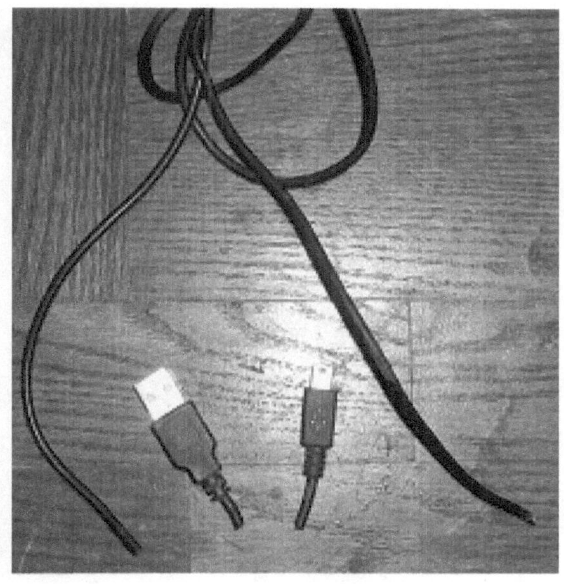

If you look closely you can see the wire in the black outer covering is small and breaks easily. This can still work, but you will need to use it the same way you would use a shoelace.

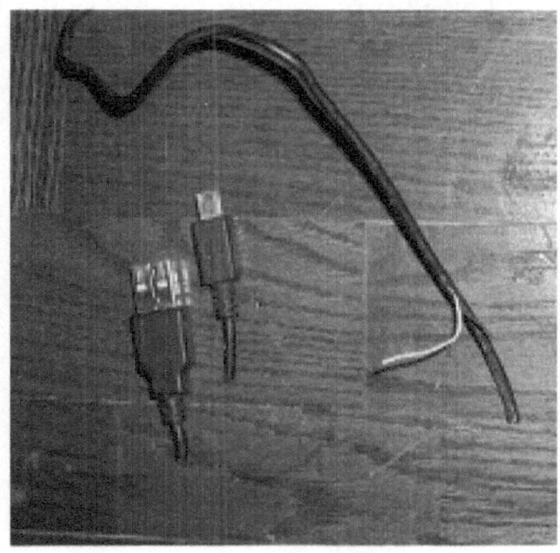

Another cord you could use this way is the earphone/earplug wires, telephone cords if you think about it there's lots of wires you could use.

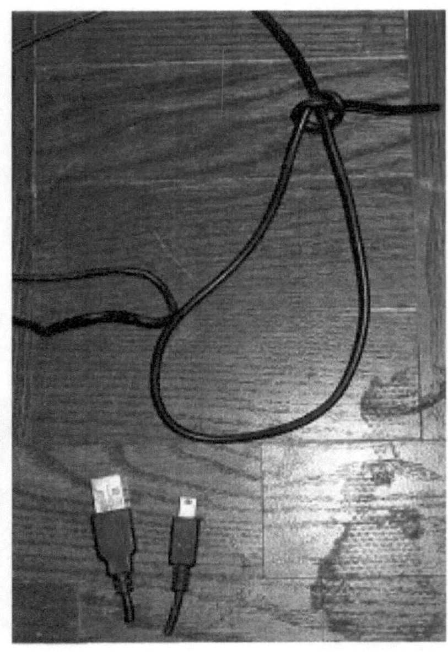

    As you can see a simple overhand knot will work, no need, to study or become an expert in knowing how to tie knots here.

    Maybe I should have pointed this out sooner its K.I.S.S. And, no I'm not talking about kissing your loved ones. It stands for **Keep It Simple Stupid**. Sorry I'm not trying to be rude here, but simple is better than complicated with everything you do. I have always been the kind of guy that believes in working smart not hard!

Yes, this is a power cord from an old computer monitor that died years ago. However, you can also use a three prong extension cord for this.

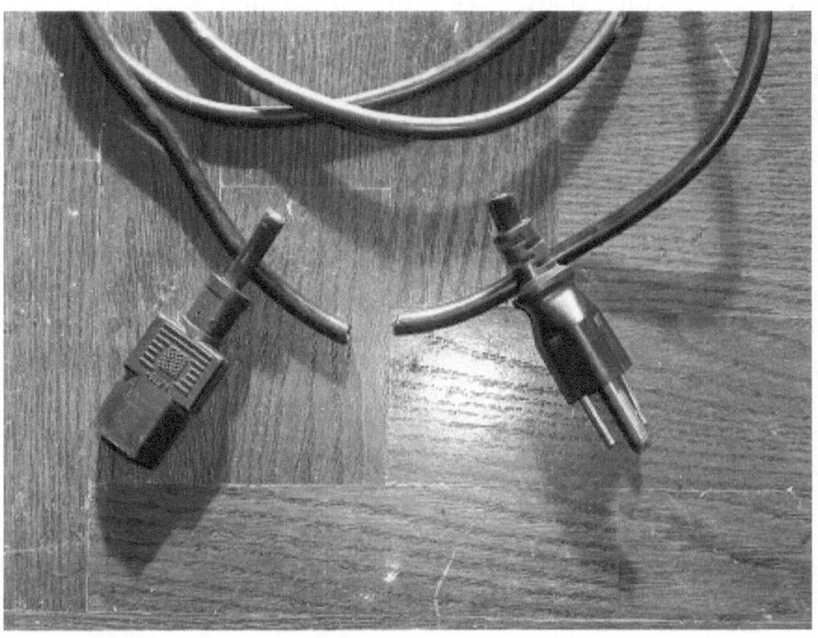

Again, you start the same way by cutting off the ends of the cord, but the wire inside is much better for making small game snares.

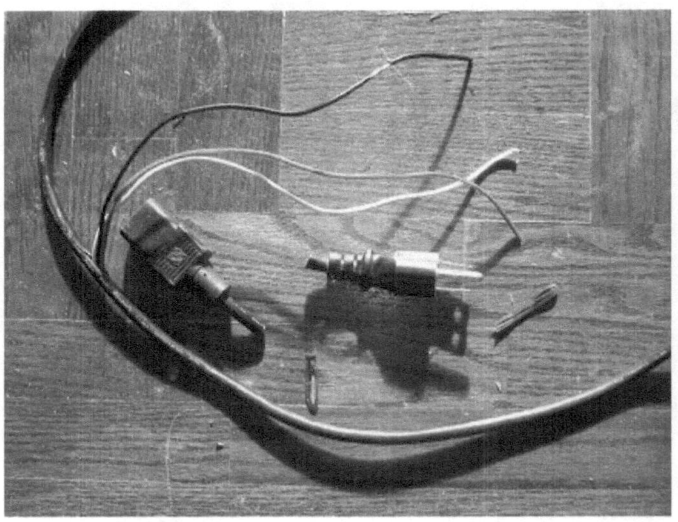

Once the ends are cut off, you need to slice the black outer cover with a sharp blade and pull the three wires out. Then you will need to take the outer cover of each individual wire. I don't recommend burning the cover off, as this will weaken the wire and it may break under the strain put on it the animal you catch.

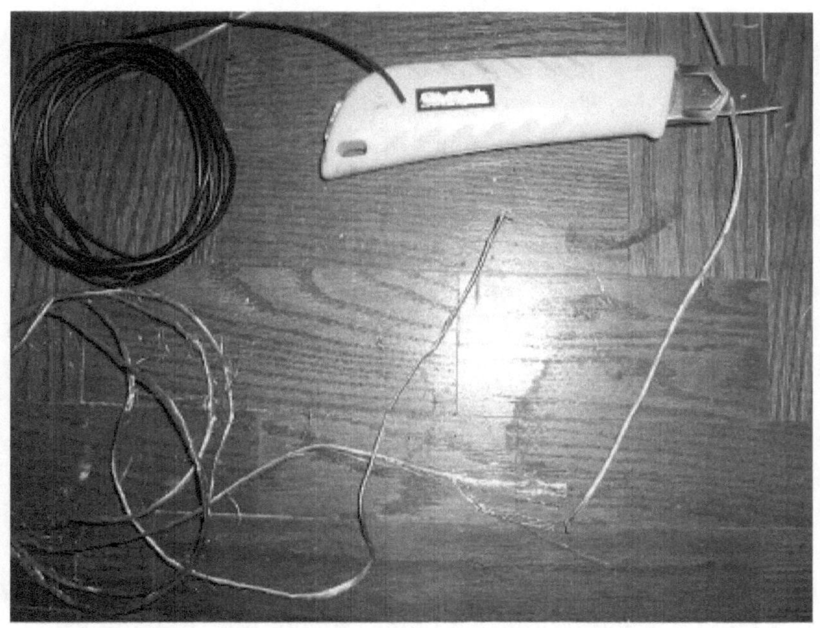

You will have to twist the wire so it doesn't come unraveled, you can also braid all three together for a much stronger snare. The ends of the wire have two loops twisted in one smaller than the other.

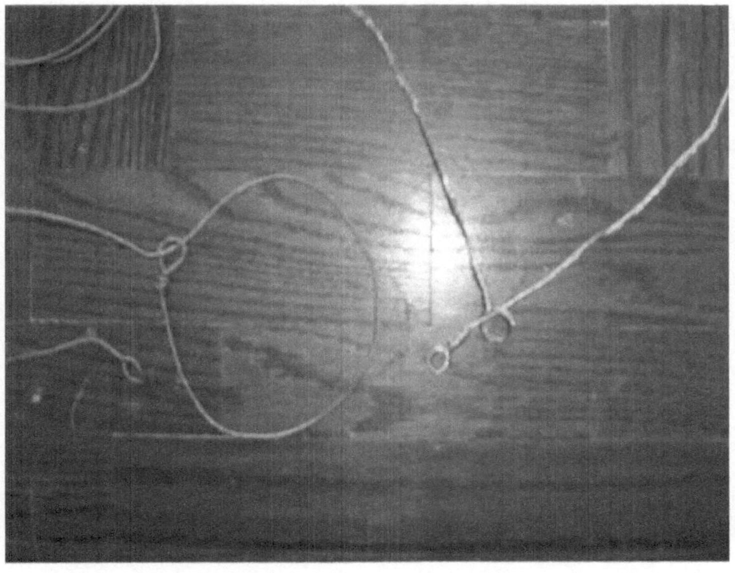

This is so you can slide the smaller one into the larger and form a noose. One end is attached to a tree or sapling and the noose is placed where the game will run into it.

About 40 years ago when I was in my 20's I had a discussion with a friend. He was a believer in the fact a snare was no good if you didn't have a tree or something to tie it to.

He went on to explain that he had found a great spot of a snare, but it didn't have a place to tie it too. So, he had to use figure 4 dead falls. Also, he said that in an open field a snare was next to useless and again, he relied on the figure 4 dead falls.

I had to agree with him as he was right, however, I don't like the figure four because you have to find and/or carry a heavy object to drop on the game. I like to work smart not hard and said there had to be a better way.

When you think about it you could find, or carry some sticks or tent pegs to push into the ground to tie off too. Why buy extra tent pegs and if you're going to spend time, looking for a stick, then you're really back to the figure four again.

No, there had to be a better way, the idea came to me that you could take a metal coat hanger, cut it in half. Bend it into an L shape with a little loop in the short end to tie you snare too. It really was that simple and it worked, however, in this day and age try to find a metal coat hanger and people looked at me as if I have two heads. Well, I did manage to find one.

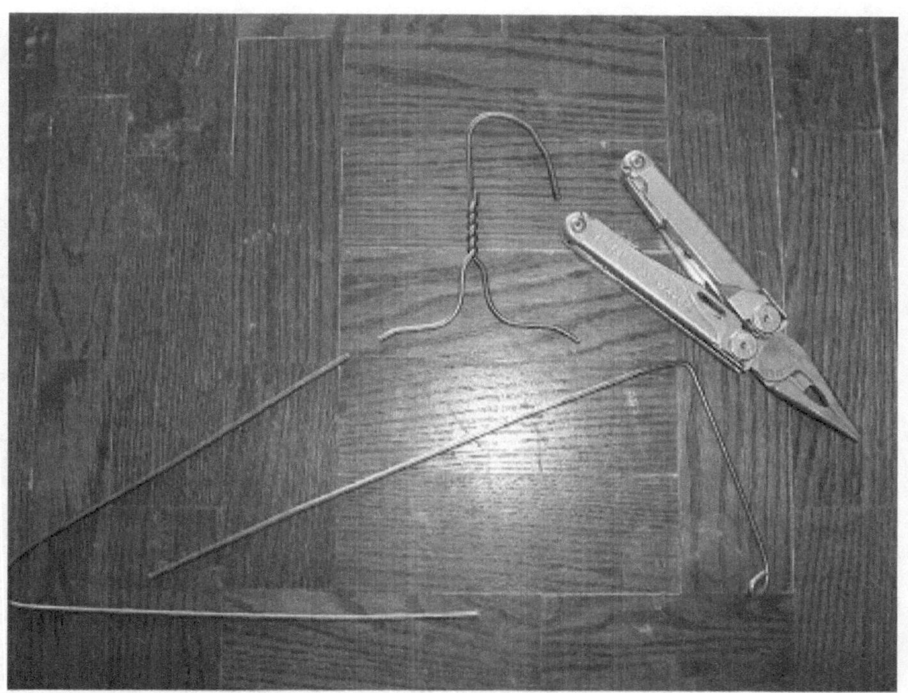

Well great ideas never dies, they just need to be modified a little. Remember life and survival is one big puzzle take what you know and rearrange it into something new or take something old and turn it into something new.

You can also use things like a bronze welding rod, and a spoke of a bike wheel they will work well for this.

This is a full spoke from a bike, I didn't even have to shorten it at all, and it's light, small and easy to carry some of them in your pocket or packsack. When you need a place to tie a snare to, you push the long end into the ground till the piece with the loop is even with the ground.

Well, my friend said it looked okay, but will it work. He took me to an industrial park later that afternoon there were lots of big warehouses and open fields. The fields had ground squirrels about the size of red squirrels that live in the fields in underground dens.

I pushed the rod into the ground and set the snare next morning we checked the snare and I had a ground squirrel, The snare loop was set to big and was wrapped around his middle so with, I care I was able to remove the snare without getting bitten or hurting him. I found him hiding as far back into his den as the snare wire would let him get. Now my friend never uses a figure four he always carries 12 of theses in his pack sack. Again, your mind is your best survival tool so use it.

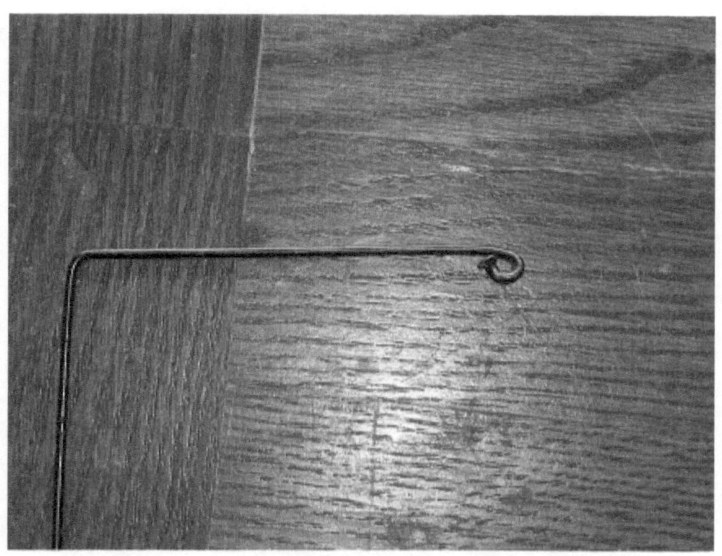

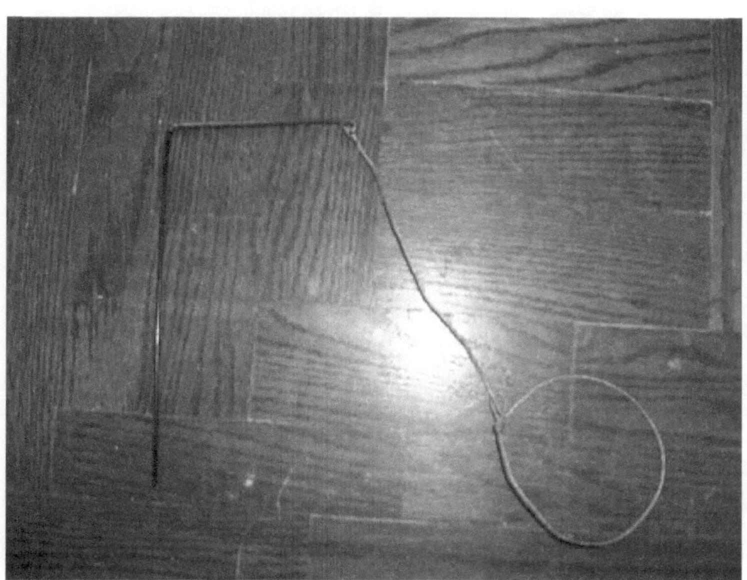

Steal jaw/leg hold traps have been around for hundreds of years and are used for fur trapping. They were made to grab a leg of the fur animal and hold it without damaging the fur. I don't use them at all they mangle small game like rabbits and I'm trapping for food not furs. However, here are so pictures so you can see what they look like.

This picture shows what they look like when they set and ready to catch an animal.

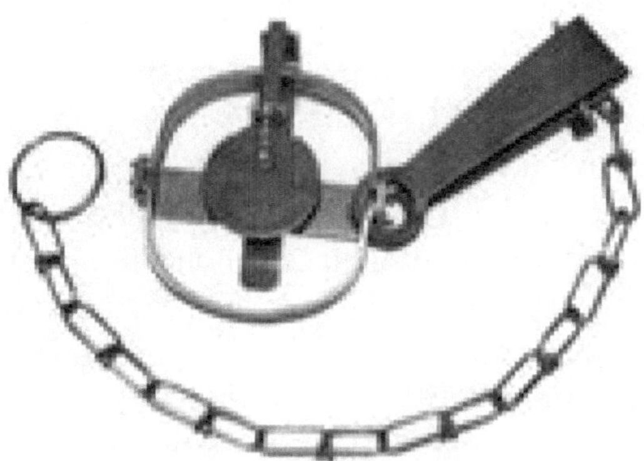

These traps use bait to lure in the animal and he steps on the trap and gets caught by the leg. The last picture is a body hold trap for small game like rabbits, it kills almost instantly.

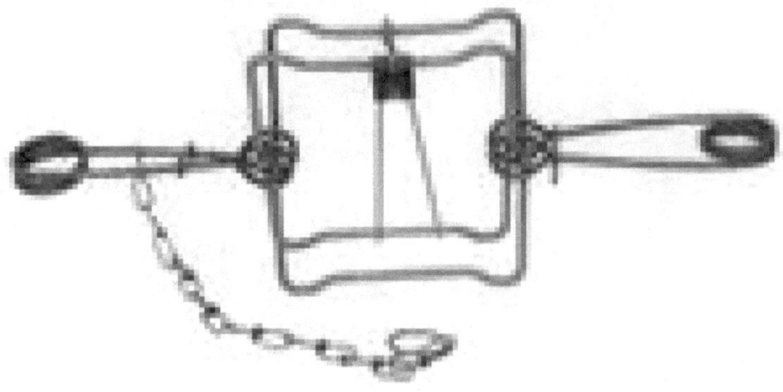

There are lots of other traps you could make but they are heavy, and it takes time to build and place them. If you're into that, build them now and store them for later if you have space, but you don't have to.

Time for another reality check with all the houses, cars, extension cords, computer wires, ear phones/plugs. You could make enough snares to supply whole armies with them. Even if you survived a plane crash, you still could use the wire from the plane to make snares.

I hear you, you can't take a knife on a plane, well, that's true, but all planes have windows and a broken piece of a window or a sharp piece of metal from the plane and you're in business. It's as simple as believing you can survive, never giving up and (using your head for more than a hat rack as my mom always told me.)

So where would you look for rabbits in the city/town/farm? Well, in your back yard, the yard next door, the school yard, the park or an industrial park. Rabbits make paths call runs they can be found along fences, buildings, and hedges. Rabbits like most game animals use cover to move from one area to another. Find the runs and place your snare so it's about 1 ½ inches off the ground in the center of the run. Just so you know rabbits have no nutritional value at all, you need other foods with rabbits to stay healthy.

Other, game you may find in city/town other than rabbits, squirrels, and pigeons are raccoons, possum, grouse, and deer as well as others. YES deer here in Winnipeg, there are small rivers as well as the red river. All have wooded areas along the banks and the deer and other animals use this to get into the city wooded park areas. Years ago a deer even got into the downtown area and animal control had to catch it and take it back to the country.

Chapter 8

Wild Plants

Yes, there's a ton of stuff I've left out most of which I don't believe are for short term disaster survival. One thing I don't know much about eatable plants.

Well, cattails (bull rushes) grow near water you can use the pollen for flour to make bread or to thicken up a rabbit soup. The young shoots and roots are eatable raw or cooked.

Lily pad leaves make a nice salad the roots can be eaten raw or cooked.

Common dandy lion leaves can be used to make salad and the roots dried and ground up make a coffee/tea of sorts and will help thicken a soup.

All oak acorns are eatable just shell them and boil them changing the water often, tasting them from time to time to see if the tannic acid is all gone. You can use them in soups or pound them to past dry and make bread.

The stinging nettle can be eaten boil the leaves and eat it like a salad you can make a tea out of the liquid. Be careful not to get stung by them; however cooking destroys the stinging stuff so it's then okay to eat or drink as a tea.

Canadian thistles the new green leaves can be eaten raw or boiled, the roots of first year plants (the really small plants) need to be peeled and can then be boiled for 30 minutes and then eaten change the water at least twice when boiling.

Clover is edible and you may even find a four leaf one for luck, Boil the flowers and new green leaves and eat them as you would spinach. Tea made from the dried flowers is also relatively high in food value.

Blue berries, strawberries

Stay away from all mushrooms it's hard to know which ones are good to eat better safe than dead!

I said I don't know much about plants, the ones I do know are easy to find and identify.

Tips and Tricks and Things I Missed

If you don't know wild rabbit and some other wild game have very little fat, you could die from just eating rabbit meat alone but there are lots of other ways we can intake fats, proteins, and vitamins in your diet. Remember you still have to try and eat a complete diet, even in a survival situation just one food source is not that good at all.

Other food sources that maybe over looked are the pet stores. Before you start in on me, yes I have try most of the foods offered there.

Not because I was hungry, but if I was going to recommend pet stores I felt I should at least sample the food. The canned foods are almost all like a patty, and the ones that say vegetable with meat and gravy are really good.

If you have bought these for your dog you know exactly what I mean. The first time I opened one I had to take another look at the label, as it look just like a can of stew we would buy for ourselves, it even tasted like a stew and it tasted great

The bagged dry cat/dog foods are okay its dry and hard with a little flavor, it can be used like a trail mix. The cat/dog treats again not to bad some are even chewy.

Bird seed bags/boxes can be eaten or used as bait for birds the seeds that are stuck together in different shapes are sweet and not that bad. Bird seeds can be boiled, or ground up for flour to make bread.

Bugs as far as I'm concerned should be used as bait for fishing. Some never the less are eatable and are a good sources of protein.

With grasshoppers take the legs off pull the head off slowly to get as much of the guts out as possible and always cook them, ether on a stick to roast or in a frying pan. The same goes for the field cricket.

Earthworms and wood grubs earth worms pinch one end and slide your fingers down the worm this will clean out the worm. Cook them in a frying pan or on a hot rock. Wood grubs you hold by the head and bite off the rest or just pull the head off and cook like the earthworm.

I would not eat other bugs and bright colored bug are never to be eaten say with the ones listed here.

Then it comes to eating remember what doesn't kill will fatten.

Now if you're looking for medicine, medical supplies, and bandages the local hospitals and walk in clinics will probable clean out right from the start. You may have better luck at the animal hospitals, clinics or animal shelters.

The only real deferent's is that the medication there is given out by so much per pound of animal. You would do the same so much for a pound per human.

Bandages at the local hospitals and walk in clinics will probable clean out right from the start as well. Again the animal hospitals, clinics or animal shelters may have been over looked.

Ladies hygiene products will make good bandages the sanitary pads for large cuts and tampons for bullet holes. You can even go where no man is supposed to go the ladies washrooms and raid the dispensers there.

You can even make bandages from clean clothes by cutting them up, folding them, and use the handy man's secret weapon duck tape, well any tape will do!

This may sound crazy but no one can walk in a straight line, we orient ourselves by seeing our surroundings and visible land marks. Like buildings, roads, and fences in a field. Take that way in the bush and you will walk in circles. The reason for this is we have a dominate side to our bodies, right handed VS left or visas versa.

So, if your right handed your right leg will be the dominate leg it will be a little stronger and push off with a little more strength, you will travel in a large circle to the left if you have no land marks to correct yourself with.

Disaster Survival!

This is what happens, to lost hunters in a heavily wooded area, where all they can see are trees in all directions and no visible land marks.

So how do we overcome this problem? We can use the sun to ordinate ourselves.

We all know that the sun comes up in the East, if we face the sun in the morning, then North is on our left shoulder, West is behind us at our back and South is off our right shoulder. Even without a compass we now know where the four cardinal directions are.

Okay, let's say we want to go North West, which would be just behind you to your left. Turn left so you're about half way between North and West, now without turning our body look back to see where the sun is. By keeping the sun in that position while walking you can now walk in a straight line to the North West.

When the sun is directly over head its noon, time to stop for an hour and have lunch. You will have to wait till around 1 o'clock for the sun to move so you can again determine where west is.

Orientate yourself to the West; North West will be just to your right and off you go again.

If you have a compass this will also help you as you won't have to stop as often to check your compass to see if you're still going the right way.

I wish I had a dollar for every time I heard someone say this doesn't look like the way we came in. The problem here is they never look back so of course it looks different.

Every 2 minutes or so have a look back the trail will look much different from the angle. So when you're on your way back you will remember seeing it that angle, and you won't say thing like this doesn't look like the way we came in.

Also when entering a clearing it's a good idea to walk 15 to 20 feet in and stop, have a good look around, so you will remember where you came in from and what it looks like.

Do you have a hunting cabin you wish had electivity? Go to a junk yard that sells good used parts and pick up an alternator and some 12 volt car batteries. Most of the new alternators have the regulators and stuff inside and can charge all 12 volt batteries as is.

Use, the fan blades from an old dead fan attach it to the alternator. You will need to put a fin of the alternator so it will turn into the wind. Get the forks of an old bike take the piece that allows the bike handles to rotate 360 degrees, and attach the modified alternator to it. Now you need to get this high enough to catch the wind above the surrounding trees.

Attach wires to the alternator run them down to your 12 volt batteries to charge them. Attach a 12 volt to 110 volt inverter and presto you have 110 alternating power.

If you have a stream close by you could make a water wheel for the alternator or you have spare cash you could get some solar cell.

You can also use the piece together solar panels for recharging the batteries on a motor home so you don't have to start the engine to recharge the batteries. By installing more batteries giving you a longer time on AC power without killing them, you can run your block heater for free on those cold winter nights.

You never know so here's the Morse Code

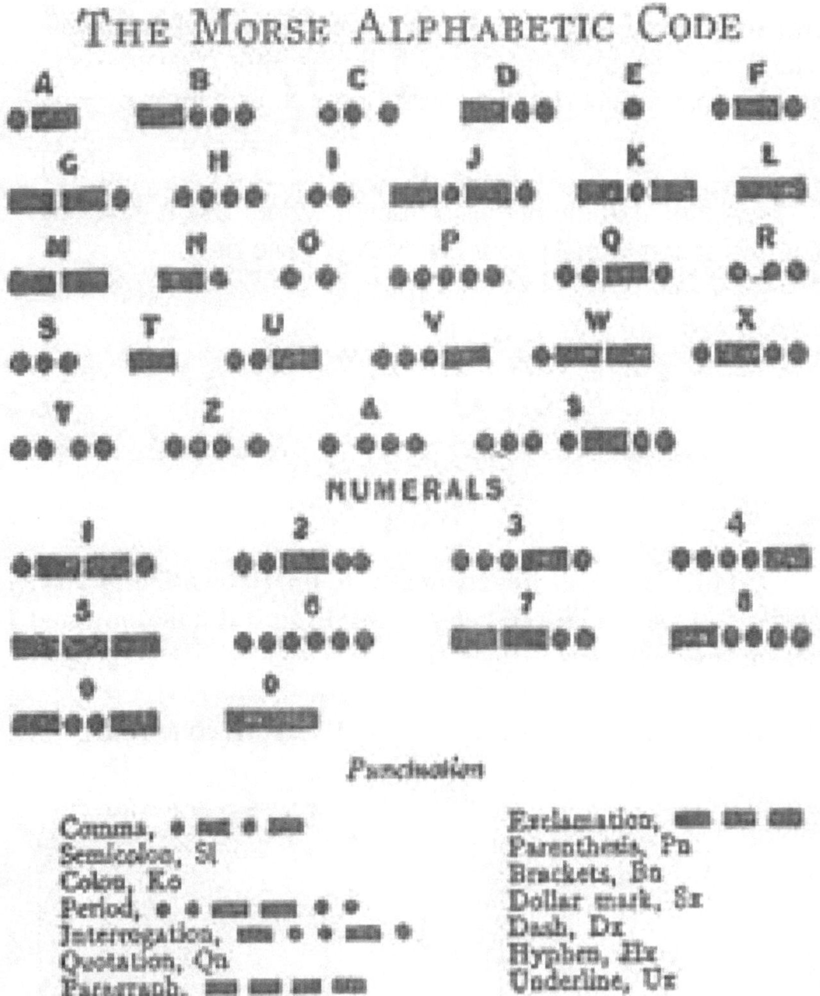

One way to signal a plane is with a mirror I'm not talking about the kind you get In an survival kit. You don't need a survival mirror when you can use any one at all.

James Evans Sr.

Hold your hand out in front of yourself at arm's length. Now hold up two fingers in the shape of a V put the plane in the center of this V and using any mirror reflect sunlight back and forth across your fingers. By keeping the plane in your finger sight the reflected light will be seen by the pilot. You can use anything that reflects light it doesn't have to be a mirror.

Again, nothing here is written in stone! Use it, rearrange the information to meet your needs as you see fit.

This book was never meant, to be, (a be all, end all) in survival. It was meant to get you thinking if it has done that I was successful.

Always remember your mind is your best survival tool!

Contents

www.ingramcontent.com/pod-product-compliance
Lightning Source LLC
Chambersburg PA
CBHW031315250726
48656CB00005B/1803